The
Novel of Violence
in America

BY W. M. FROHOCK

ARTHUR BARKER LIMITED   LONDON

Copyright © 1946, 1947, 1948, 1949, and 1950 by University Press
in Dallas

Copyright © 1953 and 1957 by Southern Methodist University
Press

Copyright © 1950 and 1957 by W. M. Frohock

All rights reserved

First edition, 1950. Second edition, revised and enlarged, 1957.

First Published in Great Britain 1959.

813.5

1 3 OCT 1959

RESERVE

b5913212

BRISTOL CITY COUNCIL
LIBRARY SERVICES
WITHDRAWN AND OFFERED FOR SALE
SOLD AS SEEN

UNIVERSITY OF WINCHESTER
LIBRARY

MADE AND PRINTED IN GREAT BRITAIN BY
MORRISON AND GIBB LIMITED, LONDON AND EDINBURGH

To LOUIS LANDRÉ

for teaching me that serious criticism begins
with the careful reading of a text

Foreword

to the second edition

I HAD INTENDED to offer this revision of *The Novel of Violence in America* with as few departures from the original edition as possible—and here and there have succeeded in doing so. Whatever opinion of Thomas Wolfe's work one held a decade ago is bound to be what one believes today, since the correspondence published in *The Letters of Thomas Wolfe* reveals, mostly, what we knew already. The same is true of the novels of Dos Passos, if for a different reason: Dos Passos' retirement from the novel leaves us exactly where we were before. And because what they have written in the intervening years reveals nothing new about them, James T. Farrell, Erskine Caldwell, and John Steinbeck now receive approximately the same treatment they received previously: a passage originally in the chapter on Wolfe has been transferred to the one on Farrell to point up a parallel between them, and an afterword on Steinbeck's most recent work now ends a study on him which is otherwise substantially unaltered. What previously was a separate examination of James M. Cain has been shortened and, because its interest is now retrospective at the best, added to the introductory chapter —in which a generally retrospective note is, at this date, unavoidable anyhow.

More radical alteration has been necessary in the cases of the writers who have remained most fully alive: Hemingway and Faulkner. The original chapter on the latter was written in reply to a type of criticism which insisted on treating him as a realist unacquainted with his own business. Criticism has since come full circle and now regards Faulkner, essentially, as an allegorist and purveyor of symbols; without accepting this as the ultimate view of Faulkner, and without discarding whatever in the earlier study has seemed to me to keep some relevance, I have reoriented the present treatment toward more current issues. In studying Hemingway I have tried to correct a critical error: while I still feel that the best of Hemingway is in the work written before 1930— and in parts of *For Whom the Bell Tolls*—I have come to feel also that my original disappointment in the later writings as a whole was too vehement and that, even if I am right in thinking that Hemingway's personality at times works at cross purposes with his intention of writing "clean, hard," and honest prose, his personality is still his own business. I have been helped toward this conclusion by the famous "Profile" by Lillian Ross in the *New Yorker*, toward which my resentment remains incandescent after several years.

Added to the text are a study of Robert Penn Warren, written since the appearance of the original edition, and two chapters which discuss aspects of the situation of the American novel at the present time. These, like the materials which made up the first version of the book, appeared first in the *Southwest Review*, and are reprinted with the permission of its publisher—who is also the publisher of the book.

W. M. F.

Cambridge, Massachusetts
October 1, 1957

Acknowledgments

I have especially to thank the late James Agee, Bert M-P. Leefmans, and Harold C. Syrett for their criticism (which I fear I have not always heeded) of the general point of view advanced in this book; Norman Torrey, Margaret Gilman, and the late Horatio Smith, for their encouragement; Joanne Mott and Allen Maxwell for patient aid with the preparation of the manuscript; and my wife for criticism, patience, encouragement, and tolerance combined.

I am indebted to the following for permission to quote from published works:

Alfred A. Knopf, Inc., for permission to reprint materials from *The Postman Always Rings Twice*, Copyright 1934 by James M. Cain.

The Houghton Mifflin Company and John Dos Passos for permission to reprint material from *Three Soldiers*, Copyright 1921; *A Pushcart at the Curb*, Copyright 1922; *Manhattan Transfer*, Copyright 1925; *U.S.A.*, Copyright 1930, 1932, 1933, 1934, 1935, 1936, 1937; and the Houghton Mifflin Company for permission to reprint a passage from *Let Us Now Praise Famous Men*, Copyright 1941.

Random House, Inc., for permission to reprint materials from *Sanctuary*, Copyright 1931; *Light in August*, Copyright 1932; *Intruder in the Dust*, Copyright 1948 by William Faulkner; and *World Enough and Time*, Copyright 1950.

The Viking Press, Inc., for permission to reprint materials from *In Dubious Battle*, Copyright 1936; *Of Mice and Men*, Copyright 1937; *The Grapes of Wrath*, Copyright 1939; *The Moon Is Down*, Copyright 1942; and *Bombs Away*, Copyright 1942 by John Steinbeck.

Charles Scribner's Sons for permission to reprint materials from *The Sun Also Rises*, Copyright 1926; *A Farewell to Arms*, Copyright 1929; *Green Hills of Africa*, Copyright 1935; *Death in the Afternoon*, Copyright 1932; *To Have and Have Not*, Copyright 1937; and *For Whom the Bell Tolls*, Copyright 1940 by Ernest Hemingway. And for permission to reprint materials from *Of Time and the River*, Copyright 1935 by Thomas Wolfe.

I am also indebted to the Vanguard Press, Inc., for the use of a passage reprinted from the Introduction of *A World I Never Made* by James T. Farrell, Copyright 1947, Vanguard Press, Inc.; to Duell, Sloan and Pearce, Inc., for the use of materials reprinted by permission of the publishers, Duell, Sloan and Pearce, Inc., from *Tobacco Road*, Copyright 1932 by Erskine Caldwell; *God's Little Acre*, Copyright 1933 by Erskine Caldwell; *Journeyman*, Copyright 1935, 1938 by Erskine Caldwell; *Trouble in July*, Copyright 1940 by Erskine Caldwell; *Tragic Ground*, Copyright 1944 by Erskine Caldwell; and to McDowell, Obolensky, Inc. for permission to reprint a passage from *A Death in the Family*, by James Agee, Copyright 1957.

W.M.F.

Contents

Contents

The Novel of Violence

in America

1
Two Strains of Sensibility

WHEN the fighting of World War II had moved northward out of the Marianas, life at USNAB Kobler Field, Saipan, became an entirely routine affair. We had comfort, a climate which encouraged inactivity, more leisure than we could use, and an admirable "ship's" library. Conditions conspired to make one reread the books he had always meant to reread. And yet, something was wrong: one kind of novel defied rereading in that atmosphere. It was easy to put down Proust and John Dos Passos and Thomas Wolfe, and hard to pick them up again; Thomas Mann and James T. Farrell were impossible.

The trouble was that we were sitting out the war in a place where, for all its attractiveness, none of us wanted to be. The hostilities to the northward might go on and on, condemning us to an indefinite term of rock-squatting. Conversation harped on the subject of time—not the undetermined time which would bring the end of the war, but the long stretch of dreary months which must pass before we would be eligible for the "rotation" which would take us back to the States. Our homesickness took the form of timesickness; we were conscious of time as the thing which stood between a man and happiness. And consequently any book in which the slow grinding of time was an important factor was intolerable to read.

3

Such a mood was manifestly incompatible with the mood in which much of the world's best fiction has been written. Consciousness of the inexorable power of time is such standard equipment of the traditional novelist that it could almost be used to define the genre. In both poetry and prose the nineteenth century had recaptured the feeling—old as Heraclitus—that nothing is eternal and that we are all victims of change. The erosion of time became a theme which gave us such figures as the two lovers who stand on a rock which is crumbling to dust, under a tree whose leaves are beginning to fall, listening to a bird which will not outlive the summer, and swear by the light of a star which is in process of burning out that they will love each other forever. In the novel it produced any number of *romans-fleuves* and "sagas"—recitals of the rise and fall which chronicle the shifting fortunes of an individual or group through many years. More recent examples of the type would include such novels, very different from each other in some ways, as *War and Peace, Buddenbrooks, Remembrance of Things Past, U.S.A.,* and *Of Time and the River.*

In spite of the inherent differences such books have marked common characteristics. Their characters tend to be passive victims who change and evolve according to the will of time, and who act less than they undergo; the real agent, the active force, is time itself. Such stories are likely to adopt a retrospective point of view, looking back to what once was and now no longer is, telescoping the span of a man's life into a few hundred pages. Their tone is frequently sad, now and then nostalgic, sometimes elegiac. Technically —as is illustrated by the elaborate devices of Proust and Dos Passos—they invite the virtuoso. At the same time, they are subject to inevitable limitation in that they permit of no catastrophe, since life as such novels perceive it permits of no dramatic conclusions. Time sweeps along and eventually the individual submerges beneath the stream, leaving his place for another; and while the character may delude himself into having a sense of his own significance, the reader is always aware that the significance is the delusion of a creature like himself, made and bounded by time. The archetype of this time-ravaged and frustrated character would probably be Flaubert's Frédéric Moreau, in the *Education sentimentale*.

It was precisely this feeling about time, and the persistent presentation of the hero as the frustrated victim of time, which, on Saipan in 1945, made it impossible to read books like *Manhattan Transfer, You Can't Go Home Again*, and the components of the trilogy about Studs Lonigan.

For the past quarter-century our favorite critical cliché had been that our literature was one of frustration and despair. We had accepted as characteristic symbols the castrated hero of *The Sun Also Rises* and the sterile landscape of *The Waste Land*. (A better one might have been the River: the passage from Ecclesiastes where Hemingway found his title involves a river which forever runs into the sea without filling it; Wolfe used the river as an explicit symbol in one book and an implicit one in the others; a river is again prominent in *Remembrance of Things Past*. In each case the stream is associated not only with time but with anguished impotence.) The mood of frustration which characterized so much that was written in America between the two World Wars involved the certainty that there was nothing new under the sun and that time must run monotonously on. We had had enough, for the moment anyhow, of time's erosions and man's defeats.

There were, however, other books as easy to read as the most anodynic detective tale. In place of *The Sun Also Rises*, for example, there was *For Whom the Bell Tolls*. In this book the role of time is completely different. Whereas in the earlier novel all days are and must be the same. Robert Jordan has four days to work out his destiny; the fourth will bring him to a conclusion, definitive and irrevocable. In this case time is not an agent working upon a character; significance lies not in what time does to the man but in what the man does in the time allotted him. Time appears as limitation. It provides a dominant sense of urgency.

Violence is epidemic in such novels. They are, like Jeffers' poems,

> Crusted with blood and barbaric omens
> Painful to excess, inhuman as a hawk's cry.

As Jordan replaces the castrated Jake Barnes, so we get Steinbeck's Casy, lying beside the water with his brains beaten out, and Frank Chambers breaking the Greek's skull with the wine bottle. In the excitement of the first perception of the two different strains of sensibility, I made the error of labeling the slow, time-obsessed one "novel of erosion," and the other, "novel of violence." The labels are too neat to be true. Most novels of the 1920's and 1930's—particularly the latter—run to violence; there is fully as much—and as horrid —in the novels of Dos Passos and Wolfe as in the later Hemingway, Steinbeck, and James M. Cain. I now prefer, for the kind of novel in which time is primarily the limit to a man's working out his fate, a somewhat pretentious-sounding but otherwise apt formula proposed by a French critic, Jean Pouillon, in his *Temps et Roman,* "novel of destiny."

For the significant distinction between the two types of fiction is not in the presence or the intensity of violence but in the fact that in the "novel of destiny" violence assumes a different aesthetic function. The hero finds himself in a predicament such that the only possible exit is through inflicting physical harm on some other human. In the infliction of harm he also finds the way to his own destruction.

But still he accepts the way of violence because life, as he sees life, is like that: violence is man's fate. Thus the pattern of this kind of novel is in a sense tragic. The hero may be defeated, but he is not frustrated. His defeat possesses meaning. And a final note of acceptance replaces the old, too familiar note of despair.

At the end of *The Sun Also Rises* Jake Barnes has nothing to look forward to except what he has seen already. The dull ache inside him has no reason not to be eternal. Time will simply run on and Jake will continue to suffer. At the end of *For Whom the Bell Tolls*, on the other hand, Robert Jordan's skein has reached its tag end: in minutes he will be dead. But his death is somehow swallowed up in victory. If in one way the victory is hollow—for Jordan becomes a victor only at the cost of his own destruction—in another the victory is complete and solid, for the emotion of victory is left in the reader. The latter knows that Jordan's death is the final affirmation of Jordan's, and his own, humanity. He has the satisfaction of knowing that Jordan is not the victim of time, but at the very worst the victim of a deluded notion of how a man should deport himself. The delusion, if delusion it is, has no importance; the significant aspect of Jordan's behavior is that a man is capable of having such a notion at all, and of living by it.

This gives a sort of satisfaction which the novel of erosion does not provide. One puts down *The Sun Also Rises* or *You Can't Go Home Again* in weariness and sadness, feeling that nothing makes very much difference anyhow. Conversely, at the end of *For Whom the Bell Tolls* or of *Light in August* one experiences a feeling of enlightenment, realizing, always as if for the first time, what man's predicament is and how gravely awful it is to be human. Since Aristotle, the spectator has always been supposed to feel some such emotion at the conclusion of a tragedy.

At their best, these tragic novels—or "novels of destiny" —conceive of violence as the characteristic mark of the human, and the acts of violence themselves are performed with great lucidity. This fact generally eluded the young Europeans who set themselves to imitating American models during and just after World War II.

At least if Camus' *The Stranger* was a fair sample, they did not grasp it. The famous murder of the Arab, which climaxes Part One of this novel, is an apt illustration of how violence can be conceived as animal. Meursault, the hero, has been presented for eighty pages as an unreflective, anaffective type, completely instinctive in his behavior. He has no resentment against the man he kills; on the rational level he has no reason for killing him. But the day is very hot, and the sun, beating down on the beach where Meursault is walking, makes him very uncomfortable. He meets the Arab and the latter, having had a fracas with Meursault's friend earlier in the day, draws a knife. The sun glints on the blade, Meursault immediately empties his revolver, and the Arab becomes a corpse. This is the tale as Meursault tells it; the metaphors he employs in his narration tell, without his being aware of it, a somewhat different story. Before meeting the Arab, Meursault, whose eyes are very sensitive, has suffered because the reflections of sunlight from the beach have been stabbing him in the eyes. The image which relates sun flash to the pointed blade recurs three times before he confronts the Arab. When the sun reflects from the Arab's knife, the flash blinds Meursault, and his heat-addled brain interprets the flash as the extension of the blade. He has thus been attacked, and he responds by reflex, as an animal responds to injury. Rationally the killing has no plausible motive. On the subrational, animal level, it is an act of violence committed in self-defense.

Compare this act of violence with the one from *In Dubi-*

ous Battle, where Mac hammers the youngster into jelly because he needs "a billboard." The cool clearheadedness with which he does the disgusting job is eloquent. Mac accepts the inevitability of what must be done; the violence is the consequence of Mac's being *who* and *where* he is, and it would be impossible for him to be *anyone* or *anywhere* else. Such violence is conceived as a part of the human condition.

The killings in Hemingway are also completely rational, human acts. When the moment comes to kill, the hero knows very clearly what he is doing and why he has to do it. Here is Harry Morgan's last murder:

Twenty-one to a clip is four bursts of five at the most, he thought. I got to be light-fingered. All right. Come on. Quit stalling, you gutless wonder. Christ, what I'd give for another one. He reached his left hand up, unhooked the length of belting, put his hand around the trigger guard, pushed the safety all the way over with his thumb and pulled the gun out. Squatting in the engine pit he sighted carefully on the base of the back of the boy's head where it outlined against the light from the binnacle.

Anything more lucid, anything less animal, would be hard to imagine—because in the context of the story the act is loaded with ethical import. It would also be hard to imagine anything less like the murder committed by Meursault.

The tragic violence in turn determines the presence in the American novels of certain special characteristics. The hero must, for example, be one who, when the chips are down, will be capable of a violent act. He will probably not belong to the middle class, because the middle class resorts less often to violence than to due process of law. Or, if like Robert Jordan he does come from the middle class, he will be estranged from his origins either by force of exterior circumstances (e.g., the economic) or by the force of personal conviction. In any case, he will figure in a plot organized in such a way as first to reveal the nature of the hero's plight, then to permit his predicament to enforce upon him the necessity of some conclusive action, and finally to make the action he takes lead him to foreseen catastrophe. The psychological makeup of the hero is, as it often is in the theater, not so much the subject as one of the data of the piece. The story must begin at a point in time so close to the moment of climax that there is no opportunity to show the *development* of character; the reader is at most allowed to recognize new aspects of character as the story progresses, but not to see the character grow, for growth does not fit in with the fundamental feeling about time.

To discuss such "novels of destiny," one is almost forced to adopt terms borrowed from the drama: "situation," "mounting tension," "climax," "resolution of tension." Inversely, certain concepts which are traditionally useful for the criticism of fiction hardly apply. One does not look in the novel of violence for "rounded" or "three-dimensional" figures; such notions as "density" or the "rich texture of life" are rarely of value. In effect, to critics who habitually measure the value of novels by such criteria, the "novel of destiny" may seem hardly to be a novel at all.

But we have heard too much, first and last, of the decadence of the novel as a literary type. Granted that the "classic" novel, as practiced by Flaubert, James, and Bourget, seems to have lost much of its vitality, there is still considerable hope. The novel is by definition "protean." Its elasticity accommodates the formal variations enforced upon it by modifications of the dominant sensibility. The critical problem is thus rather to determine the nature and formal implications of the new sensibility than to note in what circumstances the novel allegedly met its death.

There is a great temptation to elaborate a historical explanation of the emergence of the "novel of destiny." With a minimum of dramatization it could be made to appear that Wolfe and Dos Passos were the last great exploiters of the theme of time's erosions. One of them wrote a great, voluble lyric of the flight of the years; the other, with less passion and probably more intelligence, wrote their chronicle. The difference between them was the difference between obsession and self-possession. Wolfe was unpreoccupied by craftsmanship, however preoccupied he may have been with the critics who blamed him for the lack of it; the story of Dos Passos' whole development seems to be the story of a man's mastering his craft. Wolfe conceived his work largely as a problem in expression; he must at all costs say what he had to say, somehow, anyhow. Much of Dos Passos' effort, on the other hand, was expended on a preliminary intellectual conquest and assimilation of materials. In his essence, in spite of the University of North Carolina and Harvard, Wolfe gives the impression of fundamental immaturity and inadequate education, whereas Dos Passos is obviously learned in many fields and possesses a wide knowledge of the world. Wolfe was an enthusiast, but whatever one says about Dos Passos, one certainly does not allege that there was a god in him. Yet, in spite of all this, the two men were very much alike. Their material is at base the same: the effect of the passage of time, the great spectacle of futility, and the experience of being American. Both were poets, and handled their materials as poets. Both were autobiographers, fascinated by themselves and unable to keep their personalities out of their works. For each his subject finally outgrew the frame of the novel as traditionally practiced, so that each was forced to create a new frame. Between them they could be said to have exhausted the great vein of the "erosion novel."

And then what happened? Their particular attitude toward time, their consciousness of frustration and despair, like the mood of Hemingway in *The Sun Also Rises*, was characteristic of the years of the great boom. Crass American prosperity had made the expatriation of the artist almost inevitable; a lost generation slumped around the tables of the best cafés in a half-dozen European capitals and wrote for American literary reviews that were published in Paris and points east. The gloom, however comfortable, was very deep: we expected the world to end, if it ever got around to doing so, rather with a whimper than with a bang. It ended, that particular world, with a crash in 1929.

Americans went broke and contemplated—when indeed they did not join—the bread lines and the Hoovervilles, acquired social consciousness overnight, became aware of the class structure of our society and of class distinctions and of the forgotten man, got rid of prohibition and of the Republican party and of the N.A.M., and got a new deal complete with Alphabet Agencies, trouble about the Supreme Court, and a renascent labor movement. In literature, the New Humanism, the well-modulated voice of the established and cultured middle class, gave place to the strident and admittedly more cogent criticism of the Marxists; instead of Irving Babbitt we read Michael Gold, and Edmund Wilson's next book after the esoteric *Axel's Castle* was a volume of social observation based on travels around the United States. Poetry, which had been prospering in all the little reviews, went into something of a decline; the poets found their work increasingly difficult to publish. The novel, easily adjustable to new moods and climates, underwent a sea-change such that the term "novel" itself has to be very elastic to contain both the novel of the twenties and its immediate successor. Books like *The Sun Also Rises* were replaced by books like *The Grapes of Wrath*, *Tobacco Road*, *As I Lay Dying*, and, in the fulness of time, *For Whom the Bell Tolls*.

It could be argued further that the phenomenon was not exclusively American. Italy had Silone, France had Céline and Malraux, just as we had Hemingway, Faulkner, Steinbeck, Caldwell at one end of the scale, Dashiell Hammett and James M. Cain at the other. England alone did not follow suit: in 1939 it was still possible to debate whether the greatest living English novelist was E. M. Forster, whose last novel had been written a decade and a half previously, or Somerset Maugham. Meanwhile in America the new novels were succeeding at least mildly with the critics and overwhelmingly with the public at large. The most popular play of the thirties was made over for the stage from *Tobacco Road*. The serious novel which best competed with the trash in the lending libraries was Steinbeck's.

Surely there was much in the world, here and abroad, to justify the change in dominant sensibility. The depression had made us very conscious of the impermanence of our fortunes, good or bad. Violence had become the standard accompaniment of labor disputes. There was war in China, Ethiopia, and Spain, and we were facing—when we were not resolutely refusing to face—the prospect of war on a much larger scale. The thirties were the decade of Pretty Boy Floyd and John Dillinger, of Hitler, Mussolini, Franco, and Tojo. Violence was in the air, and Time's wingèd chariot was loud behind us.

How far a novel could go at that moment on little more than a knowing exploitation of violence is clear from a re-reading of writers like James M. Cain. Two things may be said of Cain with great assurance: nothing he ever wrote was completely outside the category of trash; in spite of the ultimate cheapness of his novels, an inordinate number of intelligent and fully literate people read him. He was translated in many parts of the world, and writers whose stature made him look stunted—of whom Camus in *The Stranger* is an example—paid him the compliment of imitation.

Cain calculated his effects. The preface to *Three of a*

Kind reveals how grimly he schooled himself to supercharge every sentence and jolt the reader anew on every page. He was one of the few writers then practicing in America who were really sure-handed in the manipulation of their materials. And if he wrote as he did, it was because he knew what his public wanted. The character in one of Cain's novels who got so far down on his luck that he turned "Professor" for a cathouse, playing the kind of piano the customers wanted, is almost a symbol of how Cain made a living from *his* art, with books like *The Postman Always Rings Twice*.

The Postman is Cain's book almost in the same sense that *Don Quixote* is Cervantes' book: nothing he wrote later could break down the association—he could neither live it down nor live up to it. The obvious ingredients of its success have often been enumerated, but every time we run down the list we discover something new about Cain and about ourselves. The list must always include a large item of trickery. By this I mean such devices as the one at the end of *The Postman*, where we suddenly found that what we had been reading had been written down by a condemned man in the death cell. The first-person narrative had carried us along because we had been listening to the man talk. The sentences and even the mistakes in grammar had been the sentences and mistakes of a living, human voice; the rhythms of vernacular speech had an authenticity such as is achieved only by the special talents of a Ring Lardner, or of John O'Hara at his best. The one fact the reader had become most convinced of was that Cain's hero was the kind of man who could *not*, in any circumstances, have written a story, and discovering that one has been enthralled, instead, by the *in extremis* jottings of a writer who could have made his living any time writing for M-G-M was like being caught by the rising house-lights wiping one's eyes after a particularly bathetic movie.

Today it takes very few samples like the above to persuade one that Cain worked on the assumption, justified by the facts of course, that he could do just about what he liked with the reader. The latter was a sort of victim, with weaknesses to be exploited. In *Serenade*, the hero and the Indian girl took refuge from a flash flood by breaking into a church beside the Mexico City-Acapulco road. Their copulation took place not only to the accompaniment of a roaring storm and in a Christian church but also after the girl had given way to her atavisms and appeared pagan-naked before the Christian altar. In other words, Cain was exploiting simultaneously our prurience, our instinctive fascination with sacrilege, and our curiosity about the ways of the unknown and hence glamorous savage. In *The Postman* he exploited a similar complex of unpraiseworthy instincts by having Frank and Cora relieve their passions beside the wreckage of the car which still held the body of the man they had murdered.

The scenes of his novels had much to do with the success of such legerdemain. Somehow the phoniness of *The Postman* was less phony because the action was set in and around a hamburger joint in a part of California which had magnified the tawdriness of such places until the neon light and the false front created what was almost a special cosmos. The action of the first part of *Serenade* moved through the less well-known parts of Mexico. The backdrop of *The Butterfly* was the creek-branch country of West Virginia. In each instance the setting was one unfamiliar to the reader and one where he could easily imagine curious characters like the daughter whose one purpose in life was incest, Irish steamer captains with a taste for Mozart, and Greek restaurant keepers as naïvely unsuspicious as Nick Papadakis. So long as the scene helped trick one into accepting the people, Cain had no worries. The plot would do the rest.

For the essence of the Cain novel was the plot itself. In the preface to *The Butterfly* he explained that he wrote not so much about sex, or violence, as about Pandora's box: a man wanted something terribly and took the steps necessary to get it, but when he had got it the steps could not be retraced and the thing turned out to be very harmful indeed to him. The explanation was not exactly complete. What Pandora's box contained turned out invariably to be sex, experienced always with great intensity and sometimes with just a hint of the abnormal or the taboo about it. Sex, so conceived, was inseparable from violence. Violence was both associated with the sexual act itself and made an inevitable accompaniment of anything tending to frustrate the act. In addition, violence stimulated sexual activity, as in the scene of Nick's murder. In other words, sex and violence were necessary accessories of Cain's plots.

The plots themselves were not particularly new. *The Butterfly* was a variation of the *Oedipus:* a man was involved in incest, the secret of his guilt or innocence was revealed by a mark on his body, and the catastrophe followed upon a recognition scene. *The Postman* followed the lines of an early novel of Emile Zola's called *Thérèse Raquin,* combined with a few effects straight out of Aeschylus' *Agamemnon.* What was new was not the plot material but the way the material was handled.

Cain made dialogue bear the burden of the work of telling what was on the character's mind, what he felt, what the motive was for what he had just done; it foretold what was going to happen—and by performing these functions and thus eliminating analysis and description, dialogue insured the great rapidity of the story's tempo.

She sat there a long time, twisting my hand in both of hers. "Frank, do you love me?"

"Yes."

"Do you love me so much that not anything matters?"

"Yes."

"There's one way."

"Did you say you weren't really a hell cat?"

"I said it, and I mean it. I'm not what you think I am, Frank. I want to work and be something, that's all. But you can't do it without love. Do you know that, Frank? Anyway, a woman can't. Well, I've made one mistake. And I've got to be a hell cat, just once, to fix it. But I'm not really a hell cat, Frank."

"They hang you for that."

The true subject of this passage appears in it nowhere; the "one way" is the murder of Cora's husband: to be a hell cat is to be willing to kill. She is never more specific about it than here, but she doesn't need to be. We know from the speed with which Frank understands her that the same thing has been on his mind also. On the next page they will rehearse the actual crime.

The pace of *The Postman* was properly advertised as "terrific." In the first two pages Frank had bummed a meal, seen Cora, decided to take the job Nick offered. By the end of page four he had guessed how much Cora detested her Greek husband. One more page and Frank wanted her so much he couldn't eat; another and his desire made him vomit. Some 315 lines after the start of the story Nick was in town buying a new sign and Frank was in bed with Nick's wife. Obviously, such pace could be attained only by omission of everything except what was most essential. It was characteristic of Cain's dialogue that it could bridge all the gaps and prepare the next event while the reader was still occupied with what had just happened.

The American novel had come in recent years to depend very heavily upon dialogue, and upon a kind of thought stream in an indirect discourse couched in the same language the character actually spoke. More than in any other country (certainly more than in France) the art of the novel had become dramatic—the art of dialogue. Farrell, for example, wrote so much dialogue and thought-stream monologue into his work that description and third-person narration were reduced almost to the status of stage-direction. But of all our novelists, only Hemingway did as much as Cain with as few words; and Hemingway's dialogue was frequently so concerned with the revelation of the psychology of his characters that he could not, as Cain could, entrust to it the job of keeping the story moving without third-person intervention. O'Hara had a better ear than Cain, but his dialogue existed for its own sake: we read it largely for the pleasure of hearing people as they actually talk. Cain's dialogue was lifelike only to the extent that it prevented us from saying (as we sometimes did of Farrell) that people simply did not talk like that. Once we were convinced and the illusion was established, Cain's problem was only to give us what dialogue the story required.

Clearly, dialogue like this could be used only for a certain kind of character. For complicated people with complex motives it simply would not work. But the Pandora's box plot took care of the difficulty. The character felt only one drive, to open the box. In fact, it was doubtful whether Cain cared about people at all; all he wanted was to get a box open.

There was certainly no complexity in Frank Chambers. He was a bum with muscles hardened by beating railroad detectives, one who had been in many jails. He fell for a woman and first flubbed, then succeeded in, a murder. When the pressure got heavy he ratted on his woman. Not much could bother him—although it is true that after he killed the Greek he had "those dreams." The woman he committed murder to possess went home to visit her sick mother and Frank ran off immediately with the lady who caught pumas for a living. For one thing alone he could be depended on:

as his lawyer knew, he would break when the heat was on. Otherwise, he was a pretty good shot, generally, at one-ball-in-the-side. His emotional life was stunted. His physical appetites expressed themselves without, apparently, modifying his other attitudes in any way.

A more serious novelist could have used a man like Chambers to illustrate the absurdity of life, since such a character's emotions could have been depended on never to cloud the central issue; the disparity between what he felt to be the unimportance of the acts his instincts made him commit, and the consequence attached to those same acts by society, would have stood out unobscured. But for Cain the great usefulness of this sort of character was connected not to an idea but to the way in which a man like Frank, suffering from a shortage of emotions, must pass rapidly from motive to act.

Frank Chambers killed because he had got himself in a mess. His response to stimuli was automatic and completely physical—when he wanted a woman badly enough he threw up. Love itself was indistinguishable from animal brutality and he killed what thwarted his animal need (although he did so as no animal could, calculatingly).

At this point such a character was at long remove from the Hemingway characters with whom he was frequently compared. There was nothing tragic about Frank Chambers, or about his woman. You knew about her only that she had physical attraction and that she knew she was a "cheap Des Moines trollop." Her determination "not to go back to the hash-house," and not to go on the bum with Frank, was largely a device to complete the trap Frank had got himself into—without it he would not have had to murder the Greek. She had a slight romantic-pathetic wish to be respectable and not a hell cat, but she was capable of throwing everything into the fire in a fit of jealousy. Her union with Frank was unspoiled by remorse. When her nerves got jumpy it was from insecurity, not uneasy conscience. In brief, she was what Cain's men so frequently fall for—a whore. The tragedy she and Frank concocted was tabloid tragedy, the cheap slaughter which makes only the inside pages of the thriller press.

These were figures which allowed the story to build maximum momentum. There was nothing to stop it, everything to keep it going. And for such a purpose Cain's techniques were admirable. The perspective never blurred; everything was seen through the narrator's eyes, with extreme immediacy. In the one place in *The Postman* where we had to learn indirectly what had happened—because Frank had been in a hospital bed while it was going on—we learned it from a shyster lawyer in whose dubious character we were already interested and who revealed more about himself as he disclosed each new legal machination. This, of course, was standard Cain: a Cain character, like a good Existentialist, *was* what he *did*.

And he did plenty. The "sheer speed" and "paralyzing punch" for which the publisher of the quarter edition recommended the book were largely the result of Cain's ability to eliminate gaps in the action, to develop elementary character through action, and always and forever to keep the reader off balance. One was never quite prepared for what happened. We expected Nick to get killed the first time and he didn't; we expected the second attempt to fail, but it succeeded. We thought that Frank had spilled the milk definitively when he confessed, but the amanuensis turned out not to be a policeman. We were sure Frank and Cora would get caught eventually, but we had no way to foresee that the police would get Frank only after he had killed Cora by crashing into the culvert on the way to the hospital.

The elements of a Cain novel added up to a sort of bogus

tragedy, in which ill luck took the place of fate. Perhaps here was one reason why the illusion of life was so strong in *The Postman:* luck has no place in tragedy, but it has ample scope in our daily lives. At any rate, the illusion of life was there, so strong that we accepted any number of details which, in another book, would have spoiled the reader's pleasure. Out of context there is no way to defend such paragraphs as the one following the actual killing of Nick. He has been screaming out of the window of the car in drunken delight at hearing the echo from the hills. The bottle crushes his skull just as a loud cry leaves his throat. And as Frank realizes that what they had to do has been done, the echo returns Nick's scream. The cheapness of the effect is staggering.

What made Cain's success with the reading public was his ability to appeal to the same taste which delighted in the "novel of destiny." The appeal was not legitimate, for a book like *The Postman* is thoroughly immoral—immoral not so much because of the unpraiseworthy behavior of the characters as because of the unpraiseworthy behavior of the reader. Everything in the book conspires to excite the reader to hope that somehow Frank will get away with murder, keep Cora, and elude the police. Frank Chambers does not deserve such sympathy. The reader is tricked into taking the position of a potential accomplice.

But if, instead of being a mere dose of unattenuated and immoral violence, describable in a jargon appropriate to the dignity of the story as possessing "terrific punch," Cain had produced a book of some moral seriousness, he would have given us a typical "novel of destiny." We would have had to talk about "impact" and "concentration of effect" rather than of "punch." But the books he did write did not make the grade.

The historical importance of books like *The Postman* is

2

that they were the ultimate exploitation of the climate of
sensibility which also produced the best novels of Faulkner,
Hemingway, Wolfe, Steinbeck, Farrell, and Dos Passos.
Within that climate one could discern two tendencies. The
one leaned toward combining violence of action with a feeling of time as erosive—and was productive of the kind of
fiction which was so hard to read as one sat out the months
of war on some Pacific island. The other tended toward combining time and violence in a formula of which Cain's novels
were a reduction to lowest terms. To professional historians
must be left the task of analyzing the forces which originally
brought the climate into being, and to the sociologists that
of explaining the conditions which made visions of violence
so acceptable. The concern of the chapters which follow is
with studying the American novels of violence—"novels of
erosion" and "novels of destiny" alike—which have become
part of our patrimony.

2
John Dos Passos

of time and frustration

JOHN DOS PASSOS seems to be primarily a poet who turned
to the novel because its loose construction and lack of rules
would let him do things impossible in any other form. It is
characteristic of him to try to make the novel do what it has
never done in the hands of anyone else. His mark is less the
generally high quality of his work than the immense success
of the one or two books in which he finally achieves what
he has been trying so long to do. The Frenchman Gide was
one of the same kind; after years of minor narrative writing
and study of all the potentialities of the novel, he finally
attempted one complete, full-dress job, brought it off in the
remarkably dextrous *Counterfeiters*—and never afterward
tried to do anything like it. It is as impossible to imagine
Gide writing a second *Counterfeiters* as it is to conceive of
Proust's repeating his *Remembrance of Things Past*.

This is enough to make inapplicable to Dos Passos the
very worrisome question which Hemingway raises in *Green
Hills of Africa:* why is it that American novelists eventually
peter out after brilliant beginnings? Hemingway suggests a
number of reasons, including the unfavorable effect of early
success, the corrupting influence of easy money, and the
distractions of the inevitable sojourn in Hollywood; but
nowhere does he mention the case of the novelist who feels
that he has something really new to do with the novel form,

spends years learning to do it, produces a series of books which are the record of what he has taught himself, and then at last turns out the job that crowns all the effort and justifies it. Such a man creates his own craft as he works. I am entirely unable to see how, if after this point of success he stops writing novels or turns to writing novels of a different and less successful sort, it is appropriate to assert that he has petered out. The kind of novel which compels the novelist to invent his own craft and, within the broad outlines of the genre, to create his own form, really destroys itself upon its completion. Neither this novelist nor any other can hope to exploit the same vein successfully a second time. When the *U.S.A.* trilogy was finished, Dos Passos had to turn in an entirely different direction or else spend the rest of his life copying himself.

If Dos Passos' kind of novelist really cared about cutting the best possible figure in literary histories a century from now, he should take pains to die at exactly the right time— as Proust died before he could put the finishing touches on *Remembrance of Things Past* or as Wolfe died before his prodigious cry of unmastered despair had quite reached its end. Otherwise the portrait for posterity is likely to be blurred a little by the minor writings which follow the major, as Flaubert's was by the rather regrettable ironies of his later years and as Dos Passos' will be, to some extent, by novels like *Number One* and *The Grand Design.*

Number One would have been a disappointing book even if Robert Penn Warren had not overshadowed it completely with *All the King's Men.* Its merits are considerable, but they are journalistic and not the merits of a novel. There is no good reason why Tyler Spotswood, with his ulcers and hangovers and anxiety states, should be completely trapped in his predicament, and no good reason why all the many things that happen to him have to happen. Dos Passos' picture of the Great American Demagogue is an interesting historical document, of course, but the trouble with it as fiction is that the truth is not only stranger but also more brilliant and convincing. We know that all these things have happened: that Huey Long once got beaten up in a men's room; that sound-carts are standard equipment for a certain kind of American politico; that no few of the people we elect to make our laws campaign on doctrines which would overthrow the government if ever put into practice; that in their followings have sometimes appeared some of the less ornamental members of the Christian ministry; that the great leaders sometimes have henchmen who would be their moral superiors were they not so hypnotized by the great man that when the time comes to take the rap they take it. But the Kingfish and his ilk have lived a much better picture of Number One than Dos Passos manages to produce, and Warren's study of the lad who is fascinated by the dictatorial personality probes more deeply than Dos Passos'.

It is also true that *The Grand Design* adds little to Dos Passos' stature, even though the critics who call the book weak because its author is "politically confused" carry their diagnosis farther than the facts justify. Part of the trouble may be that the maturer, quieter Dos Passos no longer experiences the consuming emotions which are the backbone of the earlier works and make the intricate structure aesthetically justifiable and necessary. They were, in a sense, the "bloody 'orse" to be controlled by the bridle and bit of technique. Without them, all the technique would be mere foolishness, *avant-garde* mannerism. In any event, *The Grand Design* cannot stand beside *U.S.A.*

But there is still no call for mourning. Dos Passos is already part and parcel of the history of our culture, and the worst that history will say about things like *Number One* and *The Grand Design* is that in addition to five fine

novels, in which he caught the spirit of his time as no one
else could, Dos Passos also wrote a number of minor books.
The really phenomenal thing would have been for him to
repeat in another direction the magnificent accomplishment
which culminates in *The 42nd Parallel, 1919,* and *The Big
Money.* To call *Number One* and *The Grand Design* evidence of petering-out is itself an indication of failure to
understand the work that preceded them.

For the man is basically a poet, with all the intense emotions of a poet, and a poet's eye. He handles his materials
as only a poet can—a poet who puts his talents to such special use that they are a help and not a hindrance in the writing of prose. I shall have little to say here about Dos Passos
as historian and as interpreter of our society, because I want
to insist on his importance as a poet and a craftsman and on
the relation of his special talents to the characteristic theme
of the novel in the era which has just closed: the theme of
human futility and of the flight of time.

To see Dos Passos as an impersonal writer is of course
not to see him whole. Much of the author's material is stuff
he has lived, a permanent part of him. Better than all the
slops and bugle calls and brutality of *Three Soldiers,* the
windows which John Andrews wretchedly washes in the
Allentown barracks sum up the misery entailed in a young
civilian's becoming a soldier. These windows reappear in
the Camera Eye parts of *U.S.A.,* and again, over a decade
later, as a casual reminiscence in *Tour of Duty.* In *Manhattan Transfer,* police invade a bohemian dancing party in
Greenwich Village and have to be called off by the district
attorney; this same incident turns up as autobiography in
U.S.A. And above and beyond all this, *U.S.A.* as a whole is
a record kept by a man who has lived in America and loved
much of it but who never, up to that point in his life, has
been able to accept it completely.

Basically Dos Passos' material, like Wolfe's, consists of reminiscence. His major effort is to summon up the memory of things past. In one book it is an event—the bald fact of a war great enough to affect the lives of a whole generation of men—that he fishes up out of the river of time: *Three Soldiers*. Then he takes a place, New York, and what it did to the people who submitted to its shaping during the first decades of the century: *Manhattan Transfer*. Finally comes *U.S.A.*, and although Dos Passos has developed his technique greatly the object is identical—to see what the same years have done to a whole country. Always his subject, like Wolfe's subject, is the years.

This is why Hollywood has kept its hands off Dos Passos, as it did for so long off Wolfe. *Moving* pictures cannot be made of the passage of time. The record of time, on film, must be kept by a series of stills. Movies call for action, and action—the picture of things happening—is not Dos Passos' line because he, like Wolfe, is interested not in happenings but rather in their effect on people. His characters are primarily victims; they do not act so much as they undergo things. In other words, his treatment of time and of people is characteristic of the novel of erosion.

The values of the world in which we now live are such that one of its finest novelists, André Malraux, confesses a great admiration for Dashiell Hammett, an admiration shared by the Olympian Gide and those most un-Olympian advocates of action, the French Existentialists. *For Whom the Bell Tolls*, the most widely read and seriously discussed novel in the America of its decade, ends in a cowboy-and-Indians scene with the hero fighting down the pain of his broken leg until he can empty his machine gun at the Fascist pursuers. And the opening tableau of *Man's Fate*, the best single novel to come out of France between the last two wars, shows a Chinese poised over a sleeping man on a mosquito-netted bed, hesitating over whether to lift the netting or to plunge the blade through netting and body at once. Whatever else this is, it is action, and it is what Dos Passos does not have.

As a Harvard man, class of 1916, Dos Passos was in Cambridge when undergraduate literary life was in a moment of great activity. His generation was roughly that of Robert Hillyer, Royal Snow, Foster Damon, John Wheelwright, and Malcolm Cowley, all of them poets and all of them very aware of the great though perhaps somewhat stifling influence of Amy Lowell. Poetry was imagism; and the current poetic doctrine made a point of seeing the world freshly. There was a vigorous sweeping away of conventional metaphor, a great impulsion to let nothing come between the eye and the object it was looking at. There was also, apparently, no small amount of undergraduate aestheticism, complete with tall candles and black drapes; but the main current was extremely serious and on the whole thoroughly beneficial. The influence of imagism was to make the young men read French, including—despite all that has been said about the impact of Laforgue and Corbière, Mallarmé and the rest— much French that was not symbolist. One whole side of imagism went back to the French Parnassians: an intense curiosity about technique, a healthy respect for workmanship, a distaste for the moralizing tone—all of which can be traced as far into the past as Théophile Gautier. This is the side of imagism that made a permanent impression on Dos Passos.

War came, and after that the years of "exile." With everyone else Dos Passos was in Europe. But his early works sound somewhat as if the war had taken place in Cambridge, Massachusetts; they are literary in the undergraduate fashion, the work of a maturing but not a mature man. In *Orient Express* and *Pushcart at the Curb* there is a streak of romantic exoticism, with the inevitable comparison of East and

West as seen by the young occidental who has come to observe himself against an Eastern backdrop and is disappointed with what he finds. He visits the various homes of romance, and romance always turns out to be an absentee. All of this is frequently unoriginal and jejune, but it has this saving grace: even as he writes Dos Passos seems to know just how immature he is. He is frankly experimental and sometimes the experiment reveals what is coming later in more important books. The last chapter of *Orient Express,* built out of shifting fantasies in the stream-of-consciousness manner then very much in vogue in the little magazines, is certainly a portent; he has finished setting down the day-by-day record of his experience in the Near East and now in the conclusion he is looking back over the past, trying to impose a form on the elusive flux of reminiscence. Later, when he has learned more about how to do it, this will be the marrow of his important books.

Meanwhile his style, here in the beginning of his work, is the style of an observer. There is no doubt that this is intentional. His interest is in the object itself, how it looked or felt or smelled. He is collecting images. There are few metaphors, either in the prose of *Orient Express* or in the verse of *Pushcart,* and those that do occur are generally made with an adjective which, in describing whatever the thing is, *identifies* it by comparison with something else. The metaphor rarely *interprets,* and there is a dearth of intellectual and emotional content, a complete absence of conspicuous rhetoric. *Pushcart* may offer few examples of durable poetry, but here is a sample of the image-maker's eye at work:

> A boy in sandals with brown dusty legs
> and brown cheeks where the flush of evening
> has left the stain of wine.
> A donkey with a jingling bell

and ears askew.
Old women with waterjars
of red burnt earth.
Men bent double under burdens of faggots.

Orient Express and *Pushcart at the Curb* are both travel books, the first of a series in which Dos Passos continually betrays the same delight in seeing things exactly. He will never lose this delight. His big novels themselves are also travel books and can be read with pleasure as such. Even in *Tour of Duty*, when he is visiting the officers' clubs of the Pacific with the other correspondents and writing a book that is full of weariness, his eyes remain unjaded and whatever he sees comes to you from the paper as fresh as if no one had seen it before. This gift of clear-sighted observation is a permanent part of his talent, which he owes to the discipline we see him practicing above in the lines from *Pushcart*.

At the same time, *Pushcart* and *Orient Express* both contain remarkable examples of a kind of paradoxical impassivity; the emotion is there, certainly, but again and again the author restrains it—as he does in *Orient Express* when he tells about the starving people who lie against the wall and the old man who snatches a piece of bread away from a famished boy who is too weak to hold it. Obviously Dos Passos is shocked, and his abstention from expressing directly the least emotion is almost ostentatious. This is again a trick, learned through the imagists, from the French poets of the middle of the nineteenth century.

And he is still following the lead of the French in refusing to develop his own ideas. We are allowed to gather that he dislikes war, the stock market, the Near East Relief, the Y.M.C.A., boosters, and all the Boyscoutery of the twenties in general. But the technique is always inferential. The reader has to draw his own conclusions. Obviously Dos

Passos conceives of himself as an artist—a conception which is itself largely a product of the nineteenth century—and it is not the business of the artist to develop ideas, much less to lecture or preach.

In this sense Dos Passos was first of all a poet and has never ceased entirely to be one. The kind of novel which we now associate with his name results from the poet's bringing to one literary form talents which are ordinarily associated with another. *Three Soldiers* is a poet's book, which succeeds for reasons not valid for the success of a novel. Out of all the antiwar books that appeared in the twenties, there is only one other which manages to summon up so much sheer hatred, E. E. Cummings' *The Enormous Room;* and this again is the work of a poet.

In other respects, *Three Soldiers* is the work of a novelist who is still learning his trade. The characters are not particularly alive and not particularly believable; you do not accept them as you do Charley Anderson and J. Ward Morehouse in *U.S.A.* And the story is not especially compelling; the final disastrous encounter with the MP's comes simply through John Andrews' own fecklessness, after he has lived through the worst of everything and has only to hang on the ropes a little longer to be clear of the Army for good. In addition to this the book, despite its name, is about one soldier. Fuselli, the San Francisco boy who ends up in a labor battalion, and Chrisfield, the southerner who finally kills an officer, are secondary figures. The foreground belongs to young, Harvard-bred, self-consciously artistic Andrews— an autobiographical character in many respects.

As Dos Passos conceives him, Andrews is another incarnation of the sensitive young man, the Clayhanger, a first cousin to Stephen Dedalus, whose story is the story of the superior person coming at the end of his adolescence into head-on conflict with institutional inertia and all the other things which threaten the sanctity of the individual. He is thoroughly frustrated.

A Hemingway character can take matters into his own hands, when he has seen violence and suffering enough, and make a private peace—there is always a Catherine Barkley and a retreat in Switzerland. He has at least retained the power to act. But when Dos Passos lets Andrews have a momentary taste of decent living and freedom, women like Jeanne (the girl from the dressmaker's shop) and Geneviève Rod provide no permanent refuge. They are at most pallia-tives. Shortly the Army reaches out to take the good life away again. Andrews has nothing left but the concentration of his rage.

He is frustrated by the Thing—in this case the war—which alters the lives of the people it involves. The people are more or less representative samples of America. Their destinies are worked out according to the terms imposed by the Thing. Meanwhile the author is there as observer, care-fully placing himself in relation to the Thing and to the people in the story. Only in this case the observer is also a character—the Camera Eye sections of U.S.A. show how often Andrews' experiences were the experiences of Dos Passos—and there is a division of intent within the novel. Consequently the reader's interest is divided between what the war does to people and the personal fate of John Andrews.

The superlative emotional tension Dos Passos achieves is the making of the book. Andrews' hatred of the war, and more specifically of the Army, is almost paranoid. At times it seems that the Army has been invented only to frustrate him. Bullied by officers and brutalized by noncoms, he moves through a military experience which takes him from the camp in Allentown to the student detachment at the Sor-bonne in an evil dream of fatigue duty, parades, bugle calls, stenches, and bad tastes. He hates the indifference of the noncoms and detests the officers who give him a sense of inferiority, and who are unconcerned about what happens to a common soldier but terribly concerned when one of their own kind is killed. The Army is one vast conspiracy to take away his liberty. He wants, in the end, nothing but to be let alone—and even this is denied him. The reader, at least the reader who knows at first or second hand the characteristic moods and attitudes of World War I, is swept along on the wave of emotion. I suspect rather strongly that those whose familiarity with war dates from the 1940's may have trouble understanding the feeling that the Army is something which molests one man and lets another alone. We missed a lot, with our universal draft and our certainty that it was merely a matter of time whether you went or not; our world was not divided into slackers and patriots; we missed the draft roundups and the slacker-hissing hysteria; but we lived in the unpleasant but confident knowledge that war had, for the time being at least, become an element in man's universal fate. The very intensity of Andrews' emotion is something that we have to make an effort to understand, but no effort at all is required to feel it.

The emotion is not, however, as expertly handled as in Dos Passos' later work. The places where Dos Passos seems to have fullest control of his materials are the ones where the imagist technique is most successful and where the emotional overtones are subordinated.

As the day brightened the mist lifted off the flat linden-green fields intersected by rows of leafless poplars. Salmon-colored houses with blue roofs wore already a faintly citified air. They passed brick-kilns and clay-quarries, with reddish puddles of water in the bottom of them; crossed a jade-green river where a long file of canal boats with bright paint on their prows moved slowly. The engine whistled shrilly. They clattered through a small freight yard, and rows of suburban houses began to form, at first chaotically in broad patches of garden-land, and then in orderly ranks with streets between and shops at the corners. A dark-grey dripping wall rose up suddenly . . .

This notation of impressions as they succeed each other in time seems to me superlatively sharp and exact, the kind of thing that some of Amy Lowell's poems aim at and that Dos Passos tries to achieve in *Orient Express* and *Pushcart at the Curb;* it is the work of the poet's practiced eye. But when Dos Passos has to face the job of conveying the emotions produced in a character by these impressions, emotions which in turn modify the impressions themselves, the amount that he has still to learn becomes apparent.

Andrews darted down a side street. He could hardly keep from shouting aloud when he found himself alone, free, with days and days ahead of him to work and think, gradually to rid his limbs of the stiff attitudes of the automaton. The smell of the streets, and the mist, indefinably poignant, rose like incense smoke in fantastic spirals through his brain, making him hungry and dazzled, making his arms and legs feel lithe and as ready for delight as a crouching cat for a spring. His heavy shoes beat out a dance as they clattered on the wet pavements under his springy steps. He was walking very fast, stopping suddenly now and then to look at the greens and oranges and crimsons of vegetables in a push cart, to catch a vista down intricate streets, to look into the rich brown obscurity of a small wine shop where workmen stood at the counter sipping white wine. Oval, delicate faces, bearded faces of men, slightly gaunt faces of young women, red cheeks of boys, wrinkled faces of old women, whose ugliness seemed to have hidden in it, stirringly, all the beauty of youth and the tragedy of lives that had been lived; the faces of the people he passed moved him like rhythms of an orchestra.

There is too much in this that is not exactly fresh: the smell rising like incense smoke that makes him hungry and dazzles him, the metaphor of the crouching cat, the dance that his shoes beat out, the ugliness of the old women, the

orchestral effect of the faces, the springy step and the clat-
tering shoes—all have something faintly secondhand about
them. Take such things out, and the rest gets up on its feet
and moves. In other words, the kind of thing that Dos Passos
does in his poems is well done here, but the human reaction
sounds ungenuine, as if he were embarrassed to pull out all
the stops. Dos Passos has here—as he will most emphatically
not have in his later work—an occasional difficulty in seeing
things through his characters' eyes.

The difficulty has its effect on Dos Passos' dialogue: *Three
Soldiers* contains some of the most stilted talk appearing in
the literature between the two wars. We are expected to
believe that Andrews and his friend Henslowe, relaxed at a
café table in Paris, talked like this:

> "And I'm going to every blooming concert... Colonne—La-
> moureux on Sunday, I know that... The only evil in the world is
> not to be able to hear music or to make it... These oysters are fit
> for Lucullus."
> "Why not say fit for John Andrews and Bob Henslowe, damn
> it?... Why the ghosts of poor old dead Romans should be
> dragged in every time a man eats an oyster, I don't see. We're as
> fine specimens as they were. I swear I shan't let any old turned-
> to-clay Lucullus outlive me, even if I've never eaten a lamprey."
> "And why should you eat a lamp-chimney, Bob?" came a
> hoarse voice beside them.

But enough. What we have here is, obviously, a good book
by a poet who is on his way to becoming a novelist: the
great over-all emotional tension and the extremely sharp
awareness of sensations are part of the poet's equipment.
In places he is momentarily a poet and nothing else, as in
all his descriptions of Paris. But at the same time we see the
characteristic Dos Passos novel taking shape. The attempt
to re-create a fragment of past time, to follow the fortunes
of a number of originally unrelated characters at once, to

hold the whole structure together by the presence of con-
tinuous emotional tension, to make the center of the novel
not a person but a Thing which conditions the lives of all the
characters, and to probe some of the sources of American
frustration—this endeavor will fructify in *Manhattan Transfer*.

Manhattan Transfer is certainly not one of those novels
that are ripped off as fast as the typewriter can pound, but
a vast and intricate job of work, written not in a fever but
in a collected calm. This fact alone is enough to set it apart
from some of the most admired novels that have been written since. Erskine Caldwell says that he wrote one of his
novels in six weeks; Faulkner reports that he took scarcely
longer to write *Sanctuary*. For all Caldwell's talent, one feels
that he has never taken time to solve the essential problem
of exactly what he is trying to do. And in much of Faulkner's
work one senses an atmosphere of improvisation. Do not
these weaknesses have some connection with the haste in
which the two men's books were written? Dos Passos takes
more time, and so does Hemingway—although it should be
added that Hemingway does not try to encompass such
staggering materials as does Dos Passos, and hardly faces so
exhausting a task. Wolfe wrestled with the angel, who from
time to time blessed him; Dos Passos wrestles with recalcitrant materials. *Three Soldiers* was a big job, although he
reduced its size somewhat, as the book progressed, by his
increasing concentration on the fortunes of John Andrews
at the expense of the other characters. Now in *Manhattan
Transfer* there are more materials and more people; the time
through which he follows them is much longer; the erosions
of time become a major ingredient in his formula, and
complicate it.

The Thing in the center of the work is now the city
instead of the Army. Dos Passos accepts, and contributes

to, the Big City myth, that particular romanticism of the metropolis exploited years ago by Zola. Zola's Paris was a living animal, and his trick of animating the inanimate—a machine like the locomotive in *The Human Beast,* or the still in *The Dram Shop,* or the mining machinery in *Germinal*—was always immensely effective. But Dos Passos sounds less like Zola than like the Chicago school, with its self-conscious delight in the brawling metropolis and its conviction that big buildings are beautiful and that the life which swarms below them is in some special way wonderful and mysterious. This convention, by Dos Passos' time very well established, has roots deep in our urban movement. Traditionally, to the man who stayed home in rural America the big city was the Babylon of vice and sin, a horrid excrescence upon the earth. To this the city man replied—being himself but recently a rural person—that everything evil said about the city was true, but that the vice and sin and general squalor were fully as lovely as they were terrifying.

There is much of the urban man's response in Dos Passos' emotion toward the city, and this emotion takes the place in *Manhattan Transfer* that hatred of the Army held in the earlier novel. His acceptance of New York as a great, lovely man-killer, indifferent to the humanity she devours, is at base romantic. The whole tone of such passages as the one in which Bud jumps off the bridge has in it the same naïve wonderment that appears in some of Sherwood Anderson's Chicago stories. There is the same sympathy with the men who have been caught in the city's jaws, mingled with fascination at the jaws themselves. Dos Passos' picture of New York is sophisticated, and drawn from the vantage point of Greenwich Village; still it is drawn to be sent home to the folks.

In his attitude toward his material, Dos Passos remains the poet we have seen in *Three Soldiers,* dependent on the

maintenance of the emotional mood to hold his book together
and frequently practicing the kind of poetry we find in all
his early books:

*Three gulls wheel above the broken boxes, orangerinds,
spoiled cabbage heads that heave between the splintered plank
walls, the green waves spume under the round bow as the ferry,
skidding on the tide, crashes, gulps the broken water, slides,
settles slowly into the slip ....*

In general feeling this seems very like Sandburg, mixed
with some of the mood of Edna St. Vincent Millay's poem
about being very tired and very merry. It makes use of the
technique Dos Passos learned at Harvard. The imagery is
built out of a succession of sense impressions, with words
like *skidding* and *gulps* which identify without interpreting.
It has the imagist's awareness of the exterior world, and the
same suppression of obvious emotions.

Yet the emotions are there, of course—the fascination
and fear and delight in the spectacle of the city coupled with
awe at the effect of the city on the people. The impact of
these emotions is carefully renewed, at the head of each
chapter, in the italicized prose poems which see the city
around the clock and through the seasons.

Meanwhile Dos Passos has learned a lot, since *Three
Soldiers,* about the trade of novel writing. From Joyce, perhaps? Is he, like Hemingway and so many others, taking
from Joyce what he finds good for his individual purpose?
Without being able to pin down anything specific in *Manhattan Transfer* as coming from *Ulysses* or from its imitators,
I think I hear the Joycean echo: "The man on the bench has
a patch over his eye. A watching black patch. A black watching patch. The kidnapper of the Black Watch, among the
rustling shrubs kidnappers keep their Black Watch. Ellen's
toes dont kick in the air."

Dos Passos puts us at the same time inside Ellen's consciousness, as she walks through the park where her mother has warned her not to go, and outside it watching her skitter along. Or take the sentence in which the half-starved and now intoxicated Bud moves with Matty the Laplander from the saloon to the brothel: "The raindark houses heaved on either side, streetlamps swayed like lanterns carried in a parade, until Bud was in a back room full of nudging faces with a woman on his knees." This is the kind of thing at which Dos Passos seemed comparatively weak in *Three Soldiers*. Now he has learned the art of working so close to the actual impact of sensations on the character that description becomes almost a sort of indirect discourse, replacing soliloquy and even, on occasion, dialogue.

Meanwhile, in comparison with *Three Soldiers*, the complexity of *Manhattan Transfer* is amazing. The main body of the story is an interwoven tangle of the biographies of Elaine, Jojo, Jimmy Herf, George Baldwin, Ruth, and all the rest. A mass of related historical material, running parallel to the narrative, is arranged to show the reader what is contemporaneous with what. A strong current of more or less hidden autobiography places the narrator in his own relation to the events, although the relation is not always clearly established. And the working of time becomes a paramount factor.

Some of the people grow up and some grow old and some of them die, while the city has its way with them all. It pulls the characters together, swirls them apart, reunites them— and each time they are older, and each time they are different: Elaine harder, Jimmy Herf more disillusioned, Gus fatter and more corrupt, Joe Harland more thoroughly disintegrated. At each reappearance you recognize them as the people you were watching a few pages back, and with the recognition comes the shock of what time has done so rapidly.

The cumulative effect of these repeated encounters with characters who are at once familiar and changed is increased not only by the italicized poems at the chapter heads, but also by the trick of quick alternations in tense between the perfect, which lets us look back upon the action, and the historical present, which makes us contemporaneous with it.

Dos Passos' handling of time involves a sort of double perspective: we grow up and develop along with the characters, and yet we are also always looking back at them from the vantage point of the 1920's. This is the chief reason that the arbitrariness of the novel is by no means bothersome. Otherwise there are more coincidences in it than a reader trained on the nineteenth century's servitude to the plausible could tolerate. To think that two dozen people coming from all over the map and moving on different social levels should meet in such intricate relationships and love, hate, fight, marry, divorce, and betray each other would else be a singular strain on the credulity. For despite what Lionel Trilling has to say in his book on Forster about the good storyteller's privilege of neglecting plausibility, it is also true that the storyteller must be really good, and know the tricks of his trade well, if he wants us to accept what is not plausible. We accept it, in the case of *Manhattan Transfer*, because in the double perspective of the novel it is as if we knew already that all these people *had* come together and we were now interested in finding out how they had done so. We have accepted the city as one of the chief actors in the piece to such a degree that we feel that if *these* people had not been brought together, others no more or less consequential would have been.

There is one character who is an exception: Jimmy Herf. And this exception points to the fact that Dos Passos has still not completely solved the problem of relating himself to the time, the place, and the events. Herf is privileged in the

sense that while we are allowed to see all the other characters as frustrated nonentities, Dos Passos wants to make us
sympathize with him and share his emotions. He is the one
who, having best seen and understood what was happening,
finally walks out on New York and all it contains. He is not
so marked an autobiographical figure as John Andrews was
in the previous book, but we cannot help feeling that he is
frequently a spokesman for Dos Passos. Yet to what extent?
And how much of what happens to Herf results from the
mere logic of the narrative and how much constitutes a special judgment on Dos Passos' part?

The relation of the author himself to the materials seems
to be the ingredient in the formula that is the least well
developed. In the kind of novel Dos Passos is writing this
problem is particularly important. The author has undergone
the same erosion of time as his fictional characters, and has
been a prey to all the forces to which they have been subjected. He was not in any way exempted; and by the very
fact of his being an artist, his natural tendency is to protest.
This protest is necessary. Without it, it is doubtful whether
his writing would have the tension that marks the work of
art. And yet—here is the dilemma—why is the plight in which
his time puts him any more significant than that in which it
—and he—puts any of his other characters? He may if he
likes place himself in the exact center of the action and show
events as happening primarily to him, but the result will be
an autobiographical character in whom interest focuses so
strongly that the other characters suffer and the unity of the
book is broken. He can neglect the others entirely, or distort
them out of all proportion—and again the effect will be to
focus attention on his own personality. Or he can, as Dos
Passos finally learns to do in *U.S.A.*, treat his own case
separately, in a part set aside from the main action of the
novel to serve as a commentary on the rest. *Manhattan*

Transfer is, among other things, excellent proof that some such expedient is requisite.

The weakness of the book—so far as I am concerned the only real weakness—comes from Dos Passos' indecision regarding his own point of view. In the chapter called "Roller-coaster," for example, just as Stan is letting himself into the apartment where in his drunken fumbling he will drench himself in kerosene and burn himself to death, we get repetitions of the prose poems at the heads of two other chapters, closely juxtaposed this time with Stan's own stream of consciousness. One is "three gulls wheel above the broken boxes," which I have quoted earlier. The other I quote now:

> *There were Babylon and Nineveh: they were built of brick. Athens was gold marble columns. Rome was held up on broad arches of rubble. In Constantinople the minarets flame like great candles round the Golden Horn . . .*

This reiteration of a sort of symphonic theme to point up a particularly tense moment in the story is, of course, effective. I suppose also that it constitutes a comment by Dos Passos on what New York does to its golden lads. But the comment at this point is an intrusion, a piece of autobiography. Stan has not seen the minarets flame round the Golden Horn; Dos Passos has—as we know from *Orient Express*. It looks very much as if the poet of the earlier book has interfered with the novelist of *Manhattan Transfer*. What the novel lacks is a firm formal arrangement of the parts which will be rigid enough to support all its material and still let the poet, the historian, and the novelist work together toward one unified effect.

In other words, *Manhattan Transfer,* for all it towers above most of the novels written in its time, is in some ways not an entirely successful experiment. The reader is always aware that some things are in the book just because Dos

Passos is trying them out: for instance, the various comic touches which smack more than a little of dada and surrealism—the Western Union messenger robbing the actor's room and carrying off all the stage money; the effeminate Oglethorpe bellowing from the fire escape through a window at his unfaithful wife; Tony Hunter chewing on Nevada Jones's carpet; the cops breaking up the "interpretative dancing" party; James Merivale starting out to make Cunningham explain the appearance of Cunningham's first and undivorced wife on the eve of his marriage to Merivale's sister, only to be frustrated because the two men meet unexpectedly at their haberdasher's and turn out to be wearing identical suits; the police dashing up after the trouble in the restaurant and hustling three uninvolved and very astonished Italo-American bystanders into the paddy-wagon. Similarly, much of the symbolism in the book seems to be there for experimental purposes: the fires, for example, which are obviously intended to be symbolic although the symbols are not entirely coherent. In *U.S.A.* such extras will have disappeared.

Here I have to insert a personal note. I belong to the generation of Americans who are least qualified to judge *U.S.A.'s* report on the first three decades of the twentieth century. We were born in the first decade, grew up during the second, went to college in the third, and became completely conscious of our surroundings only at the beginning of the 1930's. We accepted the Jazz Age because we had no standards of comparison. For all we knew, things had always been like that. And then we graduated into the Great Depression! Dos Passos' books were the first explanation we could get of our predicament, and the most compelling one. In spite of recent attempts of certain historians to rehabilitate the twenties, I find myself clinging to the belief—possibly the belief in a myth—that they were crass, crude, and corrupt indeed. To my generation *U.S.A.* occupies such a privileged position among books that we are poorly qualified to speak of it critically.

But the present discussion concerns the value of Dos Passos' poetic equipment to his novels, and his interpretation of the twentieth century has importance for the discussion only to the extent that radical liberalism informs and shapes his trilogy. Looking back from the present to Concord and beyond, one can see that America has led in the production of reformers as it has in so many other kinds of production. A century ago, men like Dos Passos and Granville Hicks might have been preaching the moral reform of society from the more liberal Unitarian pulpits, or from the Concord woods. If they had tried, for a short moment, to take a part in the Abolition movement, they would probably have withdrawn because of dissatisfaction with its practical aspects. They would have despaired at Lincoln's apparent willingness to compromise so long as compromise held promise of avoiding war. Such people act as the expression of the upwelling sense of guilt which plagues us even in our moments of greatest national complacency. We call them intellectuals, but actually they are creatures of intense emotion. And we have seen that in Dos Passos' novels strong emotional tension is the unifying factor.

The pattern of conduct of the Americans who during the early thirties tried to give up their radical liberalism for radicalism *tout court* is amazingly uniform, and forms a great testimonial to the power of conscience. The culmination of the Sacco-Vanzetti case in 1927 looked like an indication of how far the "haves" would go, even in what was supposed to be one of the most enlightened states of the Union, in desperate defense against the "have-nots." Two years later came economic collapse with its attendant suffering. Following the crash many of Dos Passos' contempo-

raries aligned themselves, emotionally if not formally, with
the people who promised to change and save the world.
Then came the great shock, the discovery that communism
was thoroughly practical, unconcerned with ethics, completely determined to have its own way at the expense of
the individual conscience. It was as inhospitable a haven for
the idealistic mind which hated compromise as the world
had yet invented. As a matter of fact, it is doubtful whether
Americans of the liberal persuasion can be happy in any
party; all parties exist for a purpose, action, and all action
is Manichean—it carries its own evil within it. This leaves
the American reformer no choice but to assume a position
of dissidence outside all parties, compromising with any and
all systems only to the extent necessary to live.

How much of this general experience Dos Passos as an
individual lived through, or what has changed his political
views so completely in recent years, is not pertinent here.
What we care about is the source of the emotion which
underlies *U.S.A.* Guided by the following Camera Eye piece
from *The Big Money*, I am identifying this source as the
conscience of the unquiet, dissident liberal, critical of America and critical of himself:

you suddenly falter ashamed flush red break out in sweat   why
not tell these men stamping in the wind that we stand on a
quicksand?   that doubt is the whetstone of understanding is too
hard hurts instead of urging   picket John D. Rockefeller the
bastard if the cops knock your blocks off it's all for the advance-
ment of the human race   while I go home after a drink and a
hot meal and read (with some difficulty in the Loeb Library trot)
the epigrams of Martial . . .

As detestation of the Army unified *Three Soldiers,* and
bemused fascination with New York unified *Manhattan
Transfer,* so here an emotion, harder to define but no less
recognizable, holds together Dos Passos' clear-eyed survey

of a situation which this time involves not one soldier-artist nor one cityful of people, but a whole country. He is mature now; he has sloughed off his occasional romanticism, foregone juvenile anger, put the irascible individual autobiographer in his proper and subordinate place. But in his maturity he is still a poet.

This may be why I have trouble accepting the view which makes Dos Passos merely a continuator of the school of French naturalists. Granted that Dos Passos has something of their great sweep, some of their ability to make a novel into an epic, a good deal of their tendency to identify the real only with the sordid, there are still many and very important differences. If Dos Passos is a naturalist at all (and the word has so many meanings that one or two of them seem almost bound to fit), he belongs to the minor naturalist connection which stems less from Zola than from the Goncourt brothers and Huysmans. He is too careful of his style, for one thing, and (how different again from Zola and Dreiser and even Thomas Wolfe!) has never fallen into the habit of such easy naturalist devices as enumeration and accumulation. He is also too much of a pessimist, whereas Zola, for all the frightfulness of his pictures of life under the Second Empire, is an incorrigible optimist—for since man's fate is determined for him by his heredity and environment, nothing is easier than to improve it by the gradual improvement of his surroundings and his blood. Dos Passos, when all is said and done, is gloomy where he is not downright bitter. His report on his life and times is anything but inspiriting. He lacks Zola's conviction that science is truth and that when we see the truth it shall make us free; he practices instead a dolorous detachment.

Again, Zola has a way of turning his characters into symbols. Nana is not merely an accomplished harlot; she represents all the rot and corruption and filth and pus of the decadent empire. The still in *The Dram Shop* is the great beast of alcoholism that feeds on men's entrails. Napoleon III, appearing at the debacle of Sedan with his cheeks rouged to hide his illness, is not merely the phony emperor but the phony empire itself. As opposed to all this, Dos Passos' characters are less symbols than samples. They are representative only in the sense that there are thousands in America like them. They represent but do not subsume. Charley Anderson and Anne Elizabeth, John Andrews and Jimmy Herf and J. Ward Morehouse are, and are meant to be, nonentities. Not one of them is anything of a hero. Or of a symbol.

The prevailing tone is ironical. The historical biographies (as opposed to the fictional biographies of which the body of the work consists) of Meester Veelson and Gene Debs, Ford, Edison, Steinmetz, and the rest, are placed in such juxtaposition to the nonentities that the entire effect is not merely one of irony but of double irony, since, despite the gap that separated a Randolph Bourne from a Ward Morehouse, the historical figures as well as the others stand in the ranks of the Defeated. In his irony as in other respects, if we are to talk of Dos Passos as a naturalist at all we must put him down among the naturalists who most closely followed Flaubert: Huysmans with his *Sac au dos* story of the conscripts who undergo all the minor vicissitudes of war but spend so much time in the eternal boredom of the troop train that the war is over before they reach the front, and Maupassant as he appears in *Boule de suif*.

Rather than talk about naturalism at all, I would prefer to carry Dos Passos all the way back to Flaubert himself. For the great influence on the American novel has been Flaubert's, however poorly he has at times been understood. A character in a Faulkner novel smells a man, and the smell is synaesthetized as being black and fluid, and his mind

immediately flies off to Flaubert's description of the death of
Emma Bovary. Hemingway talks freely of his devotion to
Flaubert and tries to adapt Flaubert's method to his own
purposes, doing with emotions what Flaubert did with
things. Farrell, in his insistence that he owes more to Zola
than he does to Flaubert, gives abundant evidence of Flaubert's general influence by knowing so terribly well whom
he does not write like! And to Thomas Wolfe, Flaubert was
an ever-present bugbear. "Flaubert me no Flauberts," he
wrote to Scott Fitzgerald, who like everyone else felt that
for Wolfe the attainment of greater precision and more rigorous selection in his writing was of the utmost importance.

Dos Passos, who seems more closely familiar with French
literature than any of the other Americans, uses one of
Flaubert's inventions as a central symbol in *Three Soldiers:*
if John Andrews ever gets out of the mess of army life he
intends to write music for the Queen of Sheba, the rich ori-
ental vision of loveliness in *The Temptation of St. Anthony.*
Andrews dwells on this until it becomes the material of all
his fantasies and the Queen comes to represent the freedom
of the artist. His preoccupation with style, his discouraged
and painful irony, his effort to maintain a kind of impassivity
or at least to let his emotion fuse his work rather than fly off
with it, his studious progress toward greater and greater control, also testify that Flaubert has never deserted him.

It even seems to me that Dos Passos is vulnerable in
U.S.A. to the same criticism once brought against Flaubert,
that at times he treats his characters with cruelty. Possibly
this is an illusion caused by the novels that have been our
fare since *U.S.A.* Hemingway, say, caresses his characters,
probably because they all have so much of Hemingway in
them. And Steinbeck—entirely incapable of producing a convincing mucker—is positively in love with some of his. In
contrast with such compassionate people Dos Passos sounds

somewhat misanthropic. He has studied the versions of the
American boob so thoroughly that his treatment seems surgi-
cal. He lacks the fund of good humor which underlies the
bitterest satire of writers like Sinclair Lewis. A capacity for
vast dislike of certain human types has always been evident
in Dos Passos' work, but in *U.S.A.* the kind of handling
reserved for the Y.M.C.A. men in *Three Soldiers* and for the
James Merivales in *Manhattan Transfer* is meted out more
or less indiscriminately. This irritates one at times, particularly since these people, as Dos Passos presents them, are
entirely incapable of being other than what they are. Mary
French, Benny Compton, Anne Elizabeth, and their like are
so completely victims of the time that they deserve a little
better than he gives them. Possibly this is the price Dos
Passos pays for having achieved a modicum of the detachment we have seen him aiming at all along, or for having
Flaubert among his models.

As is also the case with Flaubert, a large part of Dos
Passos' achievement is his triumph over technique. Of the
things we have watched him work with previously, nothing
useful has been dropped; everything is in its proper place.
The poet's eye is still at work:

daylight enlarges out of ruddy quiet very faintly throbbing
wanes into my sweet darkness broadens red through the warm
blood weighting the lids warmsweetly then snaps on
      enormously blue yellow pink
      today is Paris

This is what the Camera Eye sections are for. Elsewhere
the poet does not intrude upon the novelist. Thus the dif-
ferentiation between the characters is sharper and cleaner
cut than before: compare the pages on the death of Stan in
Manhattan Transfer with the handling of Anne Elizabeth,
as a random example, in *U.S.A.* The technical trick, of

course, is to write the biography of the character a little as
if it were in indirect discourse; Anne Elizabeth's story is
told in the language in which she herself thinks. For instance:
"He could see that Anne Elizabeth felt fine about traveling
to Rome with a real army officer who'd been to the front
and could talk Italian and everything." Or take as a still
better example the passage about the last night of Anne
Elizabeth's life when they were all in the night club: "After
they were through dancing they went into the bar to have
a gin fizz. The ceiling was hung with tricolor decoration ...
there were people singing *La Madelon de la Victoire* and
all the tough little girls were laughing and talking loud shrill
French." Now most of this second quotation might be
spoken by almost any of Dos Passos' characters, but "tough
little girls" immediately pins the thing down to Anne Elizabeth. Dos Passos' vocabulary abounds in synonyms for
"tough little girls," but none of the *mots justes,* so to speak,
are in Anne Elizabeth's vocabulary. The superb handling
of the early wanderings of Mac in *The 42nd Parallel* and of
the whole history of Joe Williams serves to show the reader
how carefully and extensively Dos Passos uses this device
in differentiating his characters. The trueness of what the
people in *U.S.A.* do, the appropriateness of the language in
which Dos Passos tells their stories, give evidence of a
remarkable mastery of a medium.

Probably the fact that the language is so extremely appropriate is the best answer to the charges of immorality sometimes leveled against Dos Passos' work. Decent people do
not talk as Joe Williams talks, or as Mac and Charley Anderson and J. Ward Morehouse talk, or behave as they behave.
Exactly! Because this kind of decency is a matter of having
had what an earlier generation called "the privileges." And
America, in the first three decades of our century, denied
these privileges—not so much by lack of money as by the

deficiencies of an entire culture—to a great many people. This, if I read him rightly, is precisely what Dos Passos is saying. Whether we agree with him or not is a different question.

In any event, the very fact of our attributing so much importance to the morality of Dos Passos is itself a tribute to the power of his work. We do not worry the same question regarding Wolfe, although his work involves the same moral problems, because Wolfe's report on America is so thoroughly personal. We are always conscious of its having been distorted in its passage through Wolfe's gargantuan personality. Dos Passos' report is different in that there is no opportunity to attribute it to the eccentricity of his view. We read Wolfe and are aware mainly of what time did to him, and of his personal feeling of frustration and futility. We read Dos Passos and are convinced of what time has done to us, and recognize the frustration and futility as our own. This position is much less comfortable for the reader, and he is prone therefore to blame the novelist who puts him in it.

"I consider John Dos Passos," wrote the French philosopher Jean-Paul Sartre some years ago, "the best novelist of our time." He sets no limits as to nationality, imposes no conditions, leaves no chance of equivocation: Dos Passos is absolutely best. I am not entirely able to subscribe to this judgment myself. Sartre, who did not then read English easily, was probably familiar only with Dos Passos' best work, whereas we in America know the less as well as the more successful books. But on the other hand, what Wolfe has done for the individual who has been frustrated and lost in his own country and swept helplessly along by time, Dos Passos has done for a whole nation. Doing it took a poet's equipment, a special training, the invention of a special form of the novel. Not much more could be asked of anyone.

3

Thomas Wolfe

time and the national neurosis

THE major part of Thomas Wolfe's effort as an artist went into trying to fix the illusory shiftings of memory before they should become lost. Again and again he spoke of his purpose as being to set down, in the time he had, his vision of life. Now, after all the years of controversy since *Look Homeward, Angel* precipitated the sterile debate which centered so often about such questions as whether Wolfe was "magnificently abundant" or "merely garrulous," the scope of his vision remains the central question about him. As he wrote to his old teacher, Mrs. Roberts, he had the Dantesque ambition to create a universe; he did not dodge the question, nor can the serious reader evade it. Every writer of course creates a universe, in the sense, at least, of having to give his characters a world in which to breathe and live. But Wolfe was self-conscious about doing it. He had ready at hand the characters to whom he was concerned to give a habitation, and this habitation is central to his vision.

One might say that he should have written of his ambition to *re*-create a universe. This would have described more accurately the process of recording a vision of the past as viewed through the distorting lens of violent and tortured temperament. "The world I create," he wrote to Mrs. Roberts, "... is always inside me." In another connection he wrote that the process of writing a novel was very n uch

52

as if a great black cloud had gathered inside him and suddenly burst. He never hid—how could he?—the very evident
fact that he was writing about himself; the unnecessary little
foreword to *Look Homeward, Angel,* in which he defends
his method on the somewhat preposterous grounds that there
is much of Swift in *Gulliver,* serves only to show how well
Wolfe knew what he was doing and how apprehensive he
was, as he would always be apprehensive, of what the critics
might say. His material was his own experience, as every
new fact we learn about him, every new letter published,
every anecdote, drives home. Under the name of Eugene
Gant or George Webber, the figure of Tom Wolfe always
stands in the center of his vision.

How completely different from Dos Passos, who was
writing at about the same time and, to a great extent, about
the same America! Dos Passos' great strength in *U.S.A.* is
his ability to maintain his own detachment. As the result of
a discipline which can be traced through his earlier books,
Dos Passos can give his reader the feeling that the events
which make up his fiction would have taken place just as
surely if there had been no novelist at hand to note them
down. His ability to establish his perspective—which he
finally achieves by the device of presenting his autobiography
as a sort of comment on the fiction—has a great deal to do
with the success of his great trilogy. Wolfe is the diametri-
cal opposite. The events of his story derive their meaning
entirely from their effect upon the central, autobiographical
character.

As Dos Passos depends essentially on a discipline which
originated in France during the middle years of the nineteenth century, Wolfe seems to go back all the way to the
English Romantics. Given the nature of his talent, it is
probably just as well that he grew up out of reach of literary modes, that he read more of Virgil than of the little

3

magazines at Asheville, that no one made him give up Melville for Henry James, that he went to the state university,
and that he reached the literary hotframe of Harvard only
after he was a man grown. He seems never to have played
the sedulous ape or to have submitted himself to the current
literary disciplines or to have acquired the writer's suspicion
of himself, of the accuracy of his own senses, or of the
validity of his report on them, which marks so much of the
literature of our time. He never acquired the constraining
awareness of the importance of technique which has conditioned men like Dos Passos. Literary sophistication simply
was not his line: who else could have written, with anything
like Wolfe's unawareness of the ludicrous side of what he
was doing, his endless variations on lines from Shakespeare?
One of his major sources of strength was that he was so
completely and miraculously out of date. "I began life," he
wrote, again to Mrs. Roberts, "as a lyric writer." He ended
life as nothing else.

Romantic lyric poetry—and we are agreed that Wolfe's
poem is romantic in many ways, including the way of revolt
—is the poetry of youth. The greatest praise we give to a
poet who in mature years writes lyrics of freshness and
originality is that he "seems so young." This strikes me as
one of the most helpful keys to Wolfe; his vision of life and
the world in which he makes his characters live are the
vision and the world of a very young man.

He felt himself so wretchedly, so miserably, and so magnificently alone. Despite all his use of the second person
plural, Eugene Gant and George Webber never escape the
feeling that their enterprises are personal and special, their
cases unique. There is a story about Wolfe, that once when
he was riding downtown after a baseball game he suddenly
alarmed a subway car by screaming, "The bastards are
ambushing me!" According to this story—which for all I

know is apocryphal—Wolfe had been talking to a friend about literary critics, but the world's series crowd on the subway did not know this, did not know Wolfe, and probably had not read his books, so that his outburst occasioned no little surprise. Now no one who has read his Wolfe faithfully would, or should, have been surprised in the least. The point is that we were all bastards—there was Tom Wolfe and then there were all the other people who were not Tom Wolfe and they were aliens. He went alone.

If his great feeling of loneliness was not pathological, it was at least exaggerated. He hated many things because they were not himself: Negroes (much of the time) and Irish Catholics (or at least the Boston Irish) and Brahmins and Jews. Eugene Gant and George Webber are repelled, immediately or eventually, by most of the people with whom they come in contact. The record of the autobiographical character's inability to establish satisfactory communication with other human beings suggests a fundamental difficulty, a failure to understand and to be understood, which may in turn be related to the state of compulsive frenzy in which Wolfe appears to have done much of his writing. With Wolfe, as with Céline, the other novelist of our time who approaches Wolfe in this matter of being repelled by people, one cannot help feeling that the drive to write, and to keep on writing at whatever cost in prolixity and reiteration, is tied up with some sort of despair of ever being fully understood.

Yet the exaggeration, painful as its results may be at times both to Wolfe and to his reader, seems only the magnification of one aspect of the time-neurosis which so generally affects Wolfe's vision and which indeed afflicts so many of the rest of us. We live, by circumstances of our birth and culture, in two periods at once and are completely at home in neither. If we do not, as Eugene Gant did, envy the English family which appears in *Of Time and the River* simply because for all their stuffiness they were so thoroughly at home where they were, or if we do not envy a man like Morison who is so sure of being understood that he converses always in ejaculations and fragments of sentences, the hero's underlying feeling of isolation, which makes him envy them, is certainly not foreign to us: transplantation implies that for a long time the plant will not take root firmly. Wolfe comes by the feeling of isolation very honestly indeed.

We have come, of late, to feel that the presence of this theme of isolation makes the mood of a novel tragic. In Wolfe's case, however, it seems clear that the exaggerated feeling of man's loneliness which permeates his work, and which conditions his whole somewhat neurotic vision of life, prevents that vision from being a truly tragic one. At this point, a comparison with the work of André Malraux becomes almost inevitable.

Wolfe and Malraux, better than any other contemporaries who come to mind, have caught up and made their own the feeling of man's solitude. Malraux's finest novel, *Man's Fate*, is full of this great loneliness which is accompanied, as it is also in Wolfe, by an almost overwhelming awareness of the imminence of death. The principal characters are beset by the problem of breaking through this loneliness into a feeling of community with their fellows. In the act of killing by stealth, Tchen is somewhat less bothered by the fact of murder than by the solitude which terrifies him as he commits it. Most of the other characters in the book experience something similar. But certain of them, at least, overcome this feeling of isolation. They go down, but they go in the knowledge that their fate is *man's* fate. And this is precisely the book which made European critics so aware of the possibilities of the tragic novel. Malraux proceeded, in

Days of Wrath, to write a novel—little known in America—which in its mood, its highly compact and concentrated form, its insistence on struggle, its atmosphere of violence, comes as near to being pure tragedy, I believe, as a novel can come. This is the story of a man imprisoned by the Nazis, whose strength to undergo imprisonment and torture and finally to escape comes from his discovering that even in the solitude of a Nazi prison no man is ever completely alone. In a preface to the book, Malraux insists that man's loneliness and man's essential solidarity are equally important; they may not be separated.

Malraux's mature awareness of the two faces to the medal is what Wolfe seems to me never to have attained. He never convinced himself that no man is an island. Wolfe's feeling of solitude—together with his awareness of the erosions of time and the imminent presence of death—appears, in comparison with Malraux's later work, as a badge of immaturity. Not that this condemns him; many writers as great as and greater than Wolfe have been immature in this sense. But their achievement has nothing to do with tragedy. The feeling of loneliness, and of the individual's being so bafflingly penned within himself, prevents it. The first person singular, as has often been remarked, is not the appropriate pronoun for tragedy.

It would be pointless, of course, to worry such a question unless in the process we got a fresh view of what Wolfe was and of what he did. It is very likely that his chronic immaturity—moral and aesthetic—warped his vision of life.

For all the lore about Wolfe—and many strange yarns are abroad about him—we really know little about him as a private person. His published letters tell us little that is not in his books. The Wolfe legend is doubtless as undependable as it is picturesque; he probably was never so colossally incapable of telling the unembellished truth about himself

UNIVERSITY OF WINCHESTER
LIBRARY

as many stories (such as the one about his persistent complaint that he was starving like Chatterton in a garret, when
actually he lived where he did only from inertia) made him
seem. In his books he sounds like one of the people—Stendhal
was another—who spend their lives trying to see themselves
as they are without ever quite penetrating the thick wall of
self-delusion.

His ability to make incredible things seem credible is
itself almost incredible. It is only when one goes back to
Look Homeward, Angel that the Aeschylean family of the
early book shows itself for what it is and the whole Pentland-
Gant clan becomes implausible if not preposterous. W. O.
Gant as Agamemnon home from the wars to die, Eliza as
Clytemnestra (her refusal to admit that there is anything
wrong with the old man being a kind of murder), Helen as
Electra when she is not doubling as Cassandra, Eugene as
the wretched Orestes . . . one feels that Wolfe cannot really
have intended these things, and yet, vaguely, there they are!
The people, if hardly the setting, of an *Oresteia*. The family
taint on which Eliza and Helen dwell is the Curse upon the
House. And on first reading, or if one has read *Look Homeward, Angel* and no more, one accepts these things unthink-
ingly; the Gant-Pentland tribe seems plausible indeed when
taken by itself.

But when one gets out of Altamont into the wider world
of *Of Time and the River*, he begins to see that too many
people are like the Gants and the Pentlands; there are simply
too many queer ducks. Robert Weaver, drinking himself
to pieces and already showing marks of the insanity "that
will destroy him"; Francis Starwick, prey of a diabolical
absence of passion; George Thornton, in the quiet depths of
whose eyes "the fatal madness which would destroy him was
already legible"; Bascom Pentland, the crazy uncle in Boston married to the crazy wife; the inordinately vulgar John

T. Brill—with such people around it is impossible not to feel
that we have strayed into some gallery of eccentrics. At times
it seems as if everyone Wolfe writes about is abnormal, or
else downright insane. And after we have seen these people
we look back at Altamont and are much less impressed by
the extraordinary population of *Look Homeward, Angel;*
the Aeschylean family now appear as only the first in a long
succession of crackpot figures. There is small doubt that
something in Wolfe's vision has warped them. All of them
are a little like the policemen who pick up Eugene and his
friends for drunken driving in a little South Carolina town.

And these huge creatures evoked for Eugene a whole history
of this earth and people, monstrous, savage, and unutterable—a
congruent and unspeakable legend which he knew, and all of
them knew, down to the roots, and which he could not speak
about and had to speak about, somehow, or die. For in these men
there was evident not only the savage and mindless energy of the
earth itself, with all that was wild, sensual, fecund, cruel and
good-natured—the whole weather of life—but there was also evident the fear, the shame, the horror that had crushed them
beneath its ocean weight of nameless and cowering dread, and
broken or destroyed their souls.

Applied to a squad of country cops, this is evidently and
clumsily out of proportion, but the fact is that Wolfe saw
most of his characters in some such light. And because of
this extravagance which works to prevent the appearance of
any group of reasonably life-size characters in his books by
which to measure the outsize of the others, those others,
the important ones, lose something of their stature, even in
Look Homeward, Angel and *You Can't Go Home Again.*

I had better open an apologetic parenthesis here to explain that, to my taste, *Look Homeward, Angel* and *You
Can't Go Home Again* are by far the best parts of Wolfe's
long novel. In spite of what I have been saying about them,

these two books, describing the preparation of Eugene's departure, and the later discovery that, as he had suspected before leaving, true return was impossible, haunt me as no other books written in America have ever done. But the other two, the story of what happened to Gant-Webber between the departure and the attempted return, seem to me less important. Possibly this is because what happens in the first and last books of the series is what happens, in some degree, to every American, whereas what happens in the middle volumes is more special; much that occurs in *The Web and the Rock* could happen only to a rising American novelist. Possibly there is another reason: it is also true that *Look Homeward, Angel* was the work of an unknown on whom the editor could exert the authority of experience, and *You Can't Go Home Again* was edited after Wolfe's death left its editor with a relatively free hand, whereas the middle volumes were products of years when Wolfe had become extremely sensitive on the subject of editing. But whatever the reason, the second and third books are spotty. Pick up any copy of *Of Time and the River* and hold the page-edges to the light; the darkened sections are sure signs that the book has been read as if it were an anthology. After the first time, one does not voluntarily read his way through the 900-odd pages of this book again. One goes directly to certain parts—some of the best writing Wolfe ever did—like the death of Eugene's father, the race between the trains, the station stop in Troy, the visit to Joel Pierce's icebox. As novels, that is to say *as wholes,* the middle books do not seem to me to stand with the other two.

Reading *Of Time and the River* directly after *Look Homeward, Angel* throws a revealing light on the people of the latter book. The Gants and Pentlands become not tragic but queer; not people working out their destiny, but frustrate victims of time. Their violence, instead of being the inevitable result of forces which drive them in a given direction, is merely the inevitable result of frazzled nerves. A typical case of this, perhaps the most eloquent that Wolfe ever invented, is the struggle between Eugene and his brother Luke, which takes place in their mother's living room. There is no point to the fight, nothing is at stake; doing physical damage to each other will accomplish no more than the temporary relief of their exasperation. This is violence without significance. Compare it with the fighting in *The Grapes of Wrath* or with the last chapter of *For Whom the Bell Tolls* and the distinction is clear. These are eccentrics clawing at each other; they are frustrated even in the attempt to do lasting harm; and this is the best proof possible that the people Wolfe sees, as he sees them, are not tragic figures.

Straightway we also doubt the reality of the places where Wolfe makes them move. Originally we accepted Altamont without question, but just as we suspect that the people are distorted as soon as we leave Altamont for Cambridge, so we also suspect Altamont itself as soon as we can put it in the new perspective. Wolfe's New England makes Altamont a never-never land.

... New England, with its harsh and stony soil, and its tragic and lonely beauty; its desolate rocky coasts and its swarming fisheries, the white, piled, frozen bleakness of its winters with the magnificent jewelry of stars, the dark firwoods, and the warm little white houses at which it is impossible to look without thinking of groaning bins, hung bacon, hard cider, succulent bastings and love's warm, white, and opulent flesh.

Harsh New England certainly is and there is no exaggerating the stoniness of its soil. Its beauty is lonely and can be tragic if you want it to be. And so forth. But New England is above all the homeland of shortage and worry, of industries that move out and of young people who emigrate because New England cannot support the children it spawns, and of old people who stay on to grub what living they can from the farms and—along the main roads—from the tourists. There is indeed a school of New England romanticists who write stuff of the "succulent bastings" sort, and there are apparently readers for it, but the difference between Wolfe's New England and the New England of people like the late Robert P. T. Coffin is that Wolfe seems actually to believe that his New England exists. It doesn't. Here where the wind is always north-northeast, as Robinson says, care is the rule —not plenty and not sensuousness. Those cozy little white houses have but one warm room in them during the winter and upstairs the chamber-pots are frozen before morning; the succulent bastings are in the writer's mind; and love's flesh is rough with goose-pimples.

Wolfe's New York is probably better. New York is at least so various that nothing said of it can be convicted of falsehood. But here again, as Wolfe watches the gray-faced, hostile millions stream through the subways, he is an outsider. There is always something about him that suggests that he is again looking in at the cozy little white houses. The intimate sentiment of New York, which Dos Passos has in spite of all the Sandburg-Millay romanticism of the big city permeating *Manhattan Transfer,* is not in Wolfe.

It is in the nature of his talent that he should see things from the outside only, and be forced always to guess what is inside them; his vision is the vision of the outsider. Thus the question naturally arises, after we have finished looking at his middle books, whether his view of Altamont is not the vision of an outsider also. Did this youth of sixteen ever read all the books Wolfe talks about, or are these the reading experiences of a mature man, garnered at the University of North Carolina; and at Harvard and thrown back in memory to be associated with the wrong age? And did the still younger lad, delivering papers in Altamont's Nigger-town, experience all its alien mystery then, or are these also the emotions of a later age thrown back upon adolescence? All these things in *Look Homeward, Angel* sound much more like a relatively older person, deep in his first work at the age of twenty-four, when he has left Altamont far behind him—as if they were a confused reconstruction of memories. No growing youth was ever quite so full of liter-ature, never felt anything with quite such transcendent keenness, any more than the Gant-Pentland family was ever quite so monstrous as Wolfe makes it look. The reconstruc-tion of the past is a notoriously tricky enterprise and Wolfe has been tricked in it.

Thus, to the earlier remark that the first person singular is not the appropriate pronoun for tragedy, we must add that the perfect is not the appropriate tense. Recollection of tragic events does not make tragedy. To get the full force of the tragic situation we need to feel contemporaneous with it; the author has to show the action as it takes place, not as it is rebuilt in retrospect. And so for this reason also Wolfe's novels are not tragic; his attitude toward his material, with special respect to time, is not a tragic attitude. It is domi-nantly emotion recollected.

But not emotion recollected in tranquillity. Wolfe's poetry is not calmly and quietly intense; his main theme is the theme of being lost in America, and it is treated by a poet who is still lost. His perspective of America itself is out of joint: distances and spaces are magnified, a trip from New York to North Carolina becomes a journey "down the continent"; much of his America is an abstraction. He has some of the naturalistic pantheism, the feeling that man and the soil are intimately bound together in essence, which marks so much Western literature since Zola and which makes him sound occasionally like Jean Giono, just as he shows at times some of the enthusiasm for being American, if not for the faith democratic, of Walt Whitman. Now and again he reveals a feeling for, though not much knowledge of, the history of our people—the feeling that this land is something apart because the dust of his ancestors is mixed with its dust. But mostly his complaint is that these things do not mean more to him than they do, that he really has no place and "no door where he can enter," and that meanwhile he is being swept along by the stream of time. The answer to his eternal question is not the answer of Whitman and Crane and Paul Engle. The one thing that he can be sure of, the one door that must open for him, is death.

Wolfe is the writer of our century who has written most eloquently about death—the death of Grover, the death of Ben, of old Gant; and of the overwhelming imminence of death everywhere. As each individual submerges beneath the river of time, something of Wolfe himself is lost; each was a parcel of his consciousness. More surely than anything else the thought of death looses that remarkable flow of his language—the unearthly torrent of words which has always been the delight of some of his critics and the bane of the rest—and also the extraordinary resources of his rhetoric.

The rhetoric is essential. One reads much more about Wolfe's breadth of vocabulary and his obviously sensuous pleasure in words, and of what someone has called his multitudinous garrulity, than about the way he used his gift. He has the distinction of being the one writer of his generation who truly dared pull out all the stops. Dos Passos cannot compete with him in this respect, because Dos Passos' method of seeing and recording impressions calls for finding the perfectly right word, and the perfectly right word is obscured if associated with a half-dozen approximately

right words; and besides, the completely successful word
for Dos Passos needs the least possible rhetorical support:
where each word stands completely for an impression the
only real linkage needed is that of consciousness, proximity
to the word which denotes the preceding impression in the
series. Hemingway cannot compete because his instinctive
emotional key, subdued and uneloquent, will not permit,
and because his favorite characters are frequently talka-
tive but rarely eloquent people.

Wolfe and his characters, on the other hand, have the
native eloquence of an old-time political orator. He needs
every resource of rhetorical structure to support the great
weight of his enormous enumerations, which are as heavy as
Dreiser's. It is extraordinary how often the rhetoric of his
own sentences is identical with the drunken rhetoric which
he puts in the sonorous mouth of the old man Gant, the
great difference of course being that Gant has the rhetorical
structure he needs, but not the words to go with it; whereas
Wolfe has the words.

The hands had given to the interminable protraction of his
living death a kind of concrete horror that it otherwise would not
have had. For as his powerful gaunt figure waned and wasted
under the ravages of the cancer that was consuming him until he
had become only the enfeebled shadow of his former self, his
gaunt hands, on which there was so little which death could con-
sume, lost none of their former rock-like heaviness, strength and
shapely power. Thus, even when the giant figure of the man had
become nothing but a spectral remnant of itself, sunk in a sorrow
of time, awaiting death, those great, still-living hands of power
and strength hung incredibly, horribly, from that spectral form
of death to which they were attached.

The words are here. And so also are most of the faults
against which the manuals of English continually warn:
prolixity, punning, cliché, repetitiousness, and the rest. What

saves it? It seems to me that in passages like this Wolfe skates determinedly around the edges of the hackneyed, rescuing himself each time through the presence of the particular word which redeems the rest and keeps the phrase from being irremediable cliché: in the first sentence "interminable protraction" saves the hackneyed "living death"; in the second, the appearance of the verb "waned"—entirely unexpected and acquiring from its context a meaning it never quite had before—stands in relation to the other verb, "wasted," as "enfeebled" stands to the rest of what would otherwise be the deadly cliché, "shadow of his former self." Such rhetorical repetitions as "spectral remnant," which picks up the earlier "shadow," and "spectral form" which in turns picks up "spectral remnant," are the sources of a freshness which is all the more perceptible because on analysis we are convinced that it comes from reviving what, except in the hands of Thomas Wolfe, would be entirely beyond hope of resuscitation.

All of this is related to Wolfe's habit of taking up some of the most familiar lines of the literary heritage and making them new and strange by the changing of a word or so: "It was unbelievable that an old cancer-riddled spectre of a man should have so much blood in him." I can remember offhand three separate places where he plays variations on the old man with so much blood in him. Despite our awareness that Wolfe abuses this device—as for that matter he abuses, sooner or later, most other rhetorical devices—its value to him is palpable. The essence of this we find in Shakespeare himself, in such lines as

> ... those blessed feet
> Which fourteen hundred years ago were nailed
> For our advantage on the bitter cross

wherein a word like "bitter," common as dirt itself, of its

own strength lifts an ordinary prose discourse into poetry. Wolfe's gift is of the same kind. The result is the sort of boldness which allows him to get away with the obvious— note the repeated pun on Gant's name in the passage above, and the association of "rock-like heaviness" with the hands of a man who has always been a stonecutter. This is the kind of eloquence that Wolfe brings to the themes of time and of death, time's child.

It is impossible to read Wolfe and like him without becoming something of an anthologist. And since each reader of Wolfe has his own favorite selections, I am offering here at least one example of his poetry of time: "... it is not the slow, the punctual sanded drip of the unnumbered days that we remember best, the ash of time; nor is it the huge monotone of the lost years, the unswerving schedules of the lost life and the well-known faces, that we remember best ..." This is the poetry of a theme on which John Dos Passos, with a poet's discipline turned to his special uses, was writing the prose.

There is no point in denying that often Wolfe let go to print much that should never have gone. Those of us who like him believe that there was a god in him, but a very unruly god who gave him no peace and at times went away without warning, as people sometimes go away and leave a radio with the switch turned on playing in an empty tenement. He was an enthusiast who had, as old Gant had, "a tragic consciousness of time," and of death. Like the people in *Look Homeward, Angel* he was a fanatic, and time and death were his obsessions. Consequently, in those moments when the god is absent he sounds like a hysterical woman who insists on feeling unloved, while life slips away without anything really stable appearing amid the flow of existence—a hysterical woman whose life is a great conspiracy to frustrate her.

Much that he wrote proves that the critics who were hell-bent to show what really needed no demonstration, i.e., that he did not know how to compose, were right, and is evidence of the compulsive frenzy in which he worked. It was often more important to him to finish saying something and get on to saying something else, than to take care for the nicety of the saying. Edward Aswell has done his best to dispel the legend that Wolfe never rewrote, and other critics who have examined Wolfe's style closely have found a change appearing in the later work; but there remains abundant proof he did not rewrite enough. Words obsess him, and rhetoric sweeps him away. Such things as Francis Starwick's having a "rather womanish" voice almost *ad infinitum,* the appearance of words like "octopal" in and out of acceptable context on so many occasions, the inability to stop ringing the changes on lines like the one about the old man with all the blood in him, the multiple repetitions of such an intuition as that Uncle Bascom's head is like Emerson's—and so on indefinitely—simply mar his work. They also testify to the great truth of Wolfe's own remark that at times when he wrote it felt as if a great black cloud had discharged itself inside him. Wolfe knew his weakness; he was haunted by the example of Flaubert, and grateful to Maxwell Perkins for assuring him that it was not necessary to be "the Flaubert kind of writer." He finally changed from Scribner to Harper in order to prove to his detractors that he, and not Maxwell Perkins, was the one who put the books together. Our criticism of him will become more cogent as we give over arguing about this incontrovertible weakness and go on to define, as precisely as we can, Wolfe's great strength.

4
James T. Farrell

the precise content

Much of Thomas Wolfe's strength lies in the fact that his multivolume poem rises out of our national neurosis of homelessness, so that his characteristic anxiety state is one that most of us have experienced in some measure. His central theme is how to adjust to life in America. But his treatment of it is only one of many possible ones, and it is thus not entirely a paradox to argue that the great strength of James T. Farrell is very similar to Wolfe's.

Wolfe's approach to the problem of adjustment can be stated simply. Much of America is still rural and many, perhaps most, Americans feel that they have rural origins. Yet our centers of culture and education are as a rule urban in spirit and sensitive to the metropolitan influence. Through them we pass in the natural process of growth, so that in the case history of the average educated American there is a record of the emotional adjustment by which the two cultures, urban and rural, have been more or less successfully brought to terms. The city is always moving ahead and the country always catching up, so that the young man coming out of the country into the city crosses not only a gap of miles but—in effect—a gap of years. We live as if in two centuries at once and belong entirely to neither; and the boy who comes from a back-eddy of Maine to the campus of a New England university, wearing his first "College Cut" suit,

69

knows as well what Wolfe is talking about as if he too had come from the hills of North Carolina.

If you are from the South, the feeling may be somewhat stronger because you are more aware of the differences. (To find a southerner who is not conscious of being a southerner is rare, whereas your Yankee, for instance, has to migrate from New England to discover that the whole world is not populated by people entirely like himself!) And Wolfe was from North Carolina. Yet the difference was of degree, not kind. The breath-taking titles themselves—*Look Homeward, Angel; Of Time and the River; You Can't Go Home Again*—point to the vast predicament in which a man finds himself trapped and frustrated because everything ebbs, flows, shifts, and refuses to be seen whole; even *The Web and the Rock* juxtaposes a suggestion of permanence with a suggestion of change. And however much his being from the South dramatized this predicament for Wolfe, the predicament itself is general.

If you grew up in the Irish South Side of Chicago, just as much as if you came out of Altamont, home is the place where you were once and where you really belonged, even though as you remember it you were not always happy there —a part of you which should have been permanent, a place where you could return after a long sojourn elsewhere. But when you actually try to go back it turns out not to be the place where, as Frost puts it, when you return they have to take you in. You have been away, having left with the premonition that coming back might not be easy, and when you try to return the place has changed and you have changed (O Lost!) and nothing is as it has been. You are, in many senses, the victim of time. Over the bridges across the culture lag traffic moves only one way.

Viewing Farrell's work in historical perspective, as the novels came off the presses, we see three volumes on the development of one individual, Studs himself. Then come two volumes (*A World I Never Made, No Star Is Lost*) in which Farrell moves his easel back and paints a broader canvas, with the primary interest shifting from character to character around a fairly large group. But then, with the third volume of the O'Neill tetralogy, a new individual begins to usurp most of the author's attention; and in the fourth the various other characters with whose fate we have been occupied retire from competition and are treated in the italicized beginnings of the chapters. Danny now takes over the main body of the narrative completely. The people who affect his life most are no longer the members of the O'Neill-O'Flaherty clans at all. We are now watching an individual who is a special rather than a typical case. The Danny O'Neill who works for his education at the University of Chicago is much less the creature of his environment than a mutation, environmentally speaking—an animal who has grown out of, and to some extent developed against the resistance of, his environment. Studs, Danny, and Farrell are about of an age. One cannot help feeling that to Farrell Studs is what but for the grace of God he might himself have been, and that Danny, having had the luck, has become to a very considerable degree an autobiographical character.

If now one looks back on the whole stretch of Farrell's Chicago story, it seems possible to say that his subject is and always has been how it feels to be a Chicago Irish-American in a world where this status subjects a man to certain disadvantages. First he treats a typical case. For two volumes he is largely preoccupied with such themes as the way in which Aunt Margaret's liaison with a minor lumber tycoon affects the emotional development of Danny and little Margaret, pushes her brother Al farther into his wistful search for cultured gentlemanliness, and warps the relationships between the wretchedly poor O'Neills and the somewhat better-off O'Flahertys. But this is only momentary, and soon the author is following the fortunes of another individual, who this time is markedly atypical, at least as compared with people like Studs, and who has a hint of autobiography about him.

As soon as Danny O'Neill emerges as the potential alien, the man estranged from the environment in which he was spawned, the immediacy of the reader's interest in the background begins to diminish. In later books, as Danny O'Neill's name changes to Bernard Clare and finally to Bernard Carr, Chicago becomes very largely reminiscence, as Altamont becomes reminiscence to Eugene Gant. It is a place which, when you are summoned back to it by an event like your father's funeral (this happens to both Gant and Carr), no longer seems very real. The New York of *The Road Between*, peopled by publishers, writers, Communist intellectuals, and the miscellaneous swarm of Greenwich Village, has no part of the clamorous, very compelling reality of the Chicago of the Lonigans and the O'Flahertys. *The Road Between* has to stand or fall by the success of Bernard Carr as character. And it is extremely difficult to make Bernard Carr succeed, if for no other reason than that the story of the young writer who is trying to find out how to write good novels and make a living and be a decent husband and keep the peace with a crowd of relatives and in-laws back home who don't especially care about being the relatives and in-laws of a novelist anyhow, is a theme on which many variations had already been played before Farrell got to it.

If we take the whole series as a sort of long, perhaps somewhat shapeless novel, the "precise content of life" is less the author's subject than is the precise content of the lives of two men, one of whom serves as foil for the other—or, effectively, the content of the life of one man. Farrell now begins to look like one of that remarkable number of writers who have felt the compulsion to put on paper, and thus to solidify and define by finding words for it, the experience of growing up in early twentieth-century America. This compulsion has something to do with the specifically American experience of living which makes one so remarkably conscious of the difference between the boy he was and the man he is, and involves some sort of leap across the gap that the sociologists like to call a culture lag. In Wolfe's case the lag seems to be a function of the differences which exist, and existed thirty or forty years ago even more markedly than they do now, between the rural and the metropolitan areas. In Farrell it pertains to the differences between the life of an underprivileged group and that of more fortunate Americans. Farrell's work, then, turns out to belong among those novels which make change the subject of special and intense contemplation, with time the agent of change and the people victims of time.

In Farrell's case there is another disturbing factor. Danny O'Neill's story is the story of a break for freedom from a repressive social and educational environment toward something more attractive. Farrell has insisted that the attraction his life as a writer offers him is the opportunity to follow an occupation where "honesty" is possible. Now what Danny is escaping to is freedom from a social situation very well summed up by the conflicting stereotypes which, by the time he has reached college, he has come to see as unperceived contradictions. He can now regard these social, moral, religious, and intellectual ambivalences as involving honesty and dishonesty. And if the crux of one's experience in life is an escape, then it would be very natural, psychologically, that the predicament from which one has escaped should come to look more terrifying than it really was; for the importance of the escape depends on one's having got away from something big. If the predicament was repressing, then its repression must look formidable—the bogey must be capable of keeping the bravest awake at night.

But it is clear from Farrell's prefaces and critical writing that this is not how he regards his own work. He has put great emphasis on his ambition to take a detached attitude toward his subject. Wolfe's admission, implicit on every page, that he is writing about himself, and Dos Passos' nice concern with arranging his own personal experience so that it forms a commentary on the stories of his imagined characters, have no parallel in Farrell. Instead he has aspired to a kind of documentary realism.

Now the "documentary" has come so thoroughly into its own in America that it is recognized as a minor but independent art. There is no question of its popularity; like most new arts it meets a general need. Its tools are word and picture, usually combined, the word either spoken or written, the picture either still or moving. Henry Luce has made a fortune with it. We have had excellent documentary movies like *The River*, excellent prose-plus-photograph work like the Steinbeck-Capa job on Russia, and excellent straight eye-witness prose like Dos Passos' wartime *State of the Nation*. From case to case the purpose may shift slightly between entertainment, education, and outright propaganda; in general it amounts to some sort of persuasion. And the persuasiveness of the documentary depends on the great authority which the public at large seems to attribute to the camera lens and to the human eye when it assumes the recording role of the lens.

The assumption that the camera does not lie is, of course, nonsense. The camera is a machine of infinite possibilities; it works with light, an extremely flexible medium, and can be manipulated to produce whatever effect the photographer wants to create. It is not a whit more reliable than the honesty of its user. The same is true of the documentary produced in words. "Photographic realism" is nothing but an infelicitous metaphor. By its nature the documentary, whether done in pictures or words, is interpretation; a piece of documentary art answers, *as one observer sees the answer,* this question: What is the precise content of life in such and such circumstances?

A paragraph in the special introduction to the reprint edition of *A World I Never Made* makes it clear that James Farrell intends his novels to answer the same question: "The problem which I was concerned with in this novel can be formulated as follows: What is the precise content of life in environments such as the environments described in this book? What does poverty mean in the intimate daily lives of those who must live in deprivation?"

This aim does not constitute Farrell's total intention, of course; he means to do other things besides. But detachment and reporting are always central in his system. Hence there is a much greater similarity of artistic purpose between a Farrell novel and a Pare Lorentz movie than there is between a Faulkner novel and a Farrell novel, for the reader approaches a Faulkner novel with the sure knowledge that what Faulkner sees will not be what any other man would see if he could occupy the same vantage point. The importance of Faulkner is the importance of his private vision, whereas the importance of the documentary, and of the novel of James Farrell to the extent that it succeeds in achieving documentary status, is that the vision is completely public.

Farrell constructs his documentary by a method familiar to anyone who has ever read a sociology book. His technique is to establish patterns of conduct. His people think in stereotypes. They live by the systematic illogic which the sociologists love. Progress on the social ladder is a question of exchanging one set of stereotypes for another. Thus Lizz

O'Neill's Catholicism is still contaminated with the various vestiges of witchcraft and magic which she has inherited from her peasant forebears (she uses Easter holy water from the neighboring Italian church because the Pope's being an Italian makes it more powerful), while her brother Al's religion is contaminated by commercial American success psychology, autosuggestion, and a touch of Christian Science. Personal destinies are largely decided by the interference between the patterns of conduct of the various individuals. Danny O'Neill is crowded out of his home, for instance, by his mother's characteristic fecundity, and his relations with his schoolmates are conditioned by his fear that they know about his aunt's drinking.

Margaret O'Flaherty's pattern is typical of the way Farrell works. Her liaison with Lorry Robinson has collapsed. So she drinks. Drinking makes her loud and she fights violently with her mother. Next she is afflicted by hangover and contrition; and at this point she generally sends some money to the Poor Clares to have them pray for her special intention. (The happiness she wants them to pray her into involves the renewal of her adultery with Lorry. For a similar moral ambivalence, compare Lizz O'Neill's refusal to practice the birth control which her religion forbids and her great willingness to take castor oil when she suspects that she is pregnant, because castor oil is really only a physic.) After her bout of contrition, Margaret may go on a renewed spree or may sober off completely. In the latter case she becomes incredibly sweet-tempered toward the people whom, when drunk, she most abuses. Shortly she is back on her job at the hotel, a fine figure of an attractive young woman, but surging full of self-pity and histrionics: the cold waters of Lake Michigan are always ready to close over her head. So when she has failed often enough to get Lorry Robinson on the phone or his letter has failed to come, sooner or later the cycle starts again—just as certainly as her sister Lizz will persist in an endless cycle of dirt, toothache, fights, prayer, eternal care of children, eternal pregnancy.

Farrell repeats the cycles, each private pattern always interfering with the others in the same way, until one comes to know these people almost intolerably well. The reader follows Aunt Margaret, drunk and sober, in her flashy clothes and in, as old Mrs. O'Flaherty says, "her pelt," until he is more intimately familiar with her than he is with his own wife and possibly understands her better. In this way Farrell manages to make the conduct of his characters completely predictable. Long before Studs Lonigan meets Catherine you know that the woman he ends up with will certainly not be his first choice, and that the union will be a result of premarital pregnancy, just as you know at the start of the World War that when the story gets up to November 11, 1918, Jim O'Neill will celebrate the coming of peace by getting into a really epic fight.

The consequence of Farrell's adopting this method is, of course, that his people become interesting in exactly the same way that the Jukes and Kallikaks are interesting. Less promising material to write novels about would be hard to find anywhere. The essence of their life is its monotony. We follow the children through the endless round of sickness, recovery, bed-wetting, pants-wetting, punishments and cuddling, home-fears and school-fears; the adolescents through myriad school experiences, athletic adventures, experiments in vice, minor crimes, fights, and scrapes; the adults through all the mechanics of earning a living, worrying, brawling, fornicating, drinking, suffering. And we observe them with a thoroughness and an intimacy that approach the clinical, until we are completely hardened to watching what happens in their beds and following them into the toilet. There is no denying that at times the work carries tremendous conviction. For example, the abject lack of privacy of the very poor comes home with a force that is almost physically painful.

Much of Farrell's success, it seems to me, can be attributed to the patient application of this sociological method.

In the France of the late 1860's Emile Zola, whom Farrell appears to admire, made a considerable stir about what he called *le document humain,* became a great taker of notes, and sometimes went to live on the scene of whatever novel he happened to be writing. By nature Zola was also something of a belated romantic poet; his novels frequently became canvases of really great scope, full of crude, inescapable symbols. His books sometimes have the sweep of Victor Hugo's poems. There seems to have been some connection between this aspect of Zola's work and the strong humanitarian passion which animated him; men could be made better, and if you improved their environment the amelioration became inevitable. All you had to do was to get rid of the repressive Second Empire and then go to work on the conditions of life.

In spite of the fact that he is too sophisticated for the transformation of men to look very easy to him, Farrell has social convictions very similar to those of Zola. He also has Zola's great faith in "document" and writes only of people and places he knows at first hand and with magnificent familiarity. But he seems to be so completely determined to turn out novels which are solid documentaries that he does none of the other things Zola did so well. Certainly the vast sweep, the impressive symbols, and the recurrent poetry of Zola do not appear in Farrell's work.

Farrell's determination to give us social realism even seems to get in the way of his using his fiction as a social weapon. A reader unaware of Farrell's social beliefs would be likely to come away from his novels with the feeling that

if there is any thesis at all in them it is much less anticapital-
istic than anti-Catholic. The Irish clergy are the real villains
of the piece. And from one point of view this is perhaps
fortunate. The forces of capitalism are largely an abstraction. To be true (and Farrell is committed to truth-to-life),
the agent of capitalism in a "proletarian" novel has most
often to be unaware of his role. On the other hand, a priest
who was not aware of his role would be the apotheosis of
improbability. Thus the priest's documentary possibilities are
much greater. The people in Farrell's novels recognize the
priest when they meet him; he is part of the precise content
of their lives. This for Farrell decides the issue—and stands
as strong testimony to the importance, from his point of
view, of producing a document.

Farrell's notion of what a document should be—a notion
obviously formed under the influence of the professional
sociologists—subjects him to several disadvantages with
which Zola never had to cope. Old-fashioned naturalism
worked on the assumption that since the human animal was
a creature of his environment, the environment deserved as
much attention as the animal it produced. Hence long and
extremely detailed descriptions, completed by direct comment from author to reader clarifying the environmental
relationship. This habit still persists in such writers as Caldwell, who here and there stops his narrative completely to
deliver himself of an essay on how his characters come to
be what they are. The old conception casts both author and
reader in the role of observer, standing quite apart from the
action and watching the behavior of the characters as it
verifies certain prestated and familiar laws. But Farrell's
persistent emphasis on the establishment of behavior patterns, with the task which this implies of differentiating
between patterns which are bound to be very much alike
anyhow, makes it necessary for him to see the action very

largely from inside the character involved. Much of the time, though not always, the reader is permitted to see no more than the character sees.

An immediate result of the technique is that the background is never very specifically Chicago, for the reason that Chicago is characteristically Chicago only by comparison with other places, and Farrell's characters are not sufficiently aware of Philadelphia, Minneapolis, or Boston to give meaning to the comparison. Consequently, while the place names—Calumet Avenue, Washington Park, and the rest —are Chicago names, there is nothing to keep the streets and houses from being equally representative of any American city large enough to have elevated tracks, heavy traffic, and crowded living conditions. The change from the older picture of the bustling, brawling young city which was so dear to the Sandburg school is in a way welcome. It permits Farrell to achieve the one sort of generality he attains; his story is less specifically the story of Chicago poor folk than it is that of poor folk anywhere in urban America where the Irish have concentrated. But in getting away from a somewhat spurious local color, Farrell has also gotten away from the kind of local color he needs. For when one is writing of the "precise content of life in given circumstances," the given circumstances had best be exceedingly specific.

In another way, the perspective that Farrell's sociological preoccupation makes him adopt is even less fortunate. Most of his story has to be told through dialogue or through the sort of indirect discourse which employs the natural language of the characters to reveal what they are thinking and how they are seeing things. The trouble here may be partly that Farrell's ear for language is not itself very keen, but his method would make the difficulty inevitable anyhow, no matter how good his ear. The unvaried social and educational background of his people makes their speech

so impressively uniform that the reader gets no respite. The
older people speak a language a bit more noticeably colored
by the old-country idiom; the younger have acquired a
good deal of the universal patter of the American tough.
Otherwise the variety is nil. Sociologically, Farrell makes
good use of his tools even here, by manipulating the language to show the real social status of the individuals. Thus
when Margaret O'Flaherty is drunk she is as foul-mouthed
as her sister Lizz, whereas sober she speaks a language befit-
ting the semigentility of her job at the hotel. But we never
forget what her social status is, for even when her spoken
language is most genteel Farrell contrives to make her
thought-stream language as low as it gets in her most
drunken moments. Even after one has appreciated this, however, it remains true that straight, old-fashioned asides to
the reader, mechanical as they are, would relieve a monotony
of language which on the whole is extremely deadening.

Asides would also take care of a psychological matter
which the indirect discourse technique fails to handle satisfactorily. The language in which the thinking of the various
characters is done does not change as the character develops.
At eighteen Danny O'Neill is supposed to be a much more
complex individual than he was at the age of ten, yet the
language in which he thinks varies from that of his thoughts
as a small boy only by being richer in the names of objects
and experiences. In the intervening years he has learned
about many new things, but he seems hardly to have per-
ceived the complexity of relationships among them.

In this particular department Farrell seems determined to
keep his work simple, and this is precisely where he would
gain by increasing its complexity. His weakness here may
reflect a basic lack of perception of the function of words
—a possibility which is also suggested, at times irritatingly,
by the adverbs which too often accompany his variants of

"he said" and "she said." Inevitably, after a speech so brimming with self-pity that no literate person could possibly miss its import, Farrell has to add: "she said, self-pityingly." Farrell is a more serious writer than James M. Cain, and deserves much more serious attention than Cain does; but at this point Cain could give him cards and spades.

The same could be said with reference to economy. Farrell not only writes dialogue in which he himself lacks confidence; he also writes too much dialogue. His people are made to talk not only poorly but also too volubly. And so, all in all, taking into consideration the loss of useful local color, the monotony of language, the shaky willingness to let the dialogue itself represent the character, and the inability to make the interior talking keep pace with the character's development, one has to admit that the essential perspective which Farrell adopts and which forces him to spend so much time "inside the character" constitutes a tall obstacle. When he does overcome it—and very frequently he does—the achievement is noteworthy. My point here is that Farrell takes this particular stance, and thus brings all this trouble upon himself, because of his determination to produce a document.

The price of making a novel "documentary" thus runs high. Is the result worth the cost?

Some years ago, Farrell and his publisher were haled into court in New York on the charge that one of his books was immoral. The judge threw the case out, on the dual grounds that this work was not dirt for dirt's sake and that conditions like those described in the book did, to his knowledge, exist. What kept Farrell from paying a serious fine was that his book was thus accepted as a documentary. One would give a lot to know what would have happened if it had been legally possible to leave out the charge of obscenity and simply try Farrell on the question of whether he really does truly report the precise content of life in the Irish South Side of Chicago. If we grant with Judge Curran that the conditions exist as described, it is still possible that the perspectives are not truthful and that they falsify the report.

As a matter of fact, the more the pages pile up, the less satisfied one is with their documentary value. The part of *Studs Lonigan* where the old folks sit around after the grammar school graduation and are unable to make conversation except in conversational stereotypes succeeds completely in convincing us of the ultimate sterility and emptiness of such lives. But after one has followed Danny's grandmother through three volumes, the repetition of her behavior pattern becomes a sort of burlesque: we know so well what the old lady will do in any situation that we laugh when she does it. And we end by feeling that she is somewhat incredible. Her inconsistencies—such as the way she hates Margaret's semiprofessional prostitution but is quite ready to share in the proceeds—finally becomes too consistently inconsistent to be believed. This is only one example. The general, over-all effect of Farrell's writing, and especially of his later work, seems to be the same.

In other words, one loses faith in the document, for the same reasons which would make it impossible to put faith in the novels of Thomas Wolfe as document. The same characters would be entirely acceptable if, presented at appropriate length, they were also frankly offered as a part of an attempt to summon up the memory of things past. Reminiscence necessarily means deformation, and in the work of a man like Wolfe one admits the necessity. In Proust, the total intention seems to be the study of the variations of appearances (the word deformation no longer quite fits because the author knows what he is up against) as these variations are determined by the passing of time. For in the "then and now" novel it is essential that not only the subject but the observer shall be a victim of time and change. Under Farrell's documentary lies an erosion novel, and the two literary types interfere.

I am also inclined to blame this confusion of auto-biography with document for Farrell's having written too much in proportion to what he has to say. The main impression one has on reading Farrell seriatim is one of bulk. The three volumes about Studs Lonigan and the four about Danny O'Neill contain several thousand pages and several million words. Add to these *Gas-House McGinty, Ellen Rogers, Bernard Clare,* and all the other stories and all the criticism, and it is clear that Farrell has already produced more than most writers do in a lifetime.

He has done all this producing at a moment when critics as a race are developing a considerable, and probably justifiable, prejudice against bulk, because bulk suggests a pandering to the public taste for busty heroines and lusty adventure, carried on long enough to give people plenty of paper for their money. It also suggests hasty writing—and we are still in the grip of the great Flaubert myth, which persuades us that it is impossible to write much and well at the same time. Actually Flaubert, in writing so little, was an exception among novelists. The general rule has been that the great ones are the great producers: Dickens, Zola, Scott, Balzac, some of the Russians. It would be a shame to under-estimate Farrell merely for the bulk of his work. I am not at this point joining in the general hue and cry; Farrell certainly never meant his novels to be gulped down at the rate of one a night, anyhow. I am talking about their bulk merely because I think I recognize in Farrell's garrulity the same sort of affliction that beset Wolfe.

Wolfe never could finish talking about his own experience. He changed publishers; he changed heroes; but changing his subject was beyond him. And his style is the only testimony needed that he never got said what he wanted to say. There is a suggestion of the same phenomenon in what Farrell tells us about how, allowing almost no lapse of time after finishing *Studs Lonigan*, he went back to work on what became the story of Danny O'Neill. Why so soon, this return to the same documentary material and the same experience of life, if not that he too is a victim of that same compulsion to turn one's own past over and over, endlessly, without being able to come to any fixed, solid, basic understanding of its meaning? The three volumes of *Studs Lonigan* were already a respectable document. But it looks very much as if, after he had finished one three-volume report on the precise content of his life in a certain place, Farrell then set out—in effect, though perhaps not knowingly—to write four more which would establish his own relationship to these same events and people. There is a certain unsureness in this, similar perhaps to the unsureness which makes him distrust the effectiveness of his dialogue. The result is a document which is certainly exaggerated, an autobiography entrammeled by the document, and a bulkiness which can never be completely justified.

All this puts Farrell a stride or two behind writers like Wolfe and Dos Passos. But his deep moral seriousness still makes it impossible to shrug him off as one shrugs off, for example, half of Steinbeck. And his ability to make living people rather than puppets makes him superior to Caldwell. Read in small pieces, his novels have real power. Only when one considers them in their total effect is one aware that something is, and always has been, a little wrong.

4

5
Mr. Warren's Albatross

ROBERT PENN WARREN has written four novels, all of which teem with violent action: *Night Rider* (1938), *At Heaven's Gate* (1941), *All the King's Men* (1945), and *World Enough and Time* (1950). On the four he has built an impressive reputation. It is saying nothing new to remark that he is one of the few first-rate novelists to emerge in the United States recently.

The novels are only a fraction of his literary work. He began as one of the Nashville Fugitive poets, and has written poetry which is eminently respectable—although quite possibly more respected than read. Since the early thirties he has been an active critic, publishing frequently in the since defunct *American Review* and later in such literate little quarterlies as the *Sewanee Review* and the *Kenyon Review*. Accordingly he is identified both with the professional Southerners and the "new" (i.e., close-to-the-text, remote-from-all-else) critics, and in this latter connection has received the accolade of wrath from traditionalist literary scholars such as Professor E. E. Stoll. As a teacher he has confected, in collaboration with Cleanth Brooks, what is unquestionably the most useful manual extant for teaching the young to read poetry. And between times he has also held a Rhodes scholarship, written a strange biography of John Brown (1929), published a collection of short fictions, *The Circus in the Attic* (1948), and one narrative poem, *Brother to Dragons* (1953), taught in several colleges, and helped edit several magazines.

Warren, therefore, is that very rare phenomenon among American writers, a successful novelist who is also a sophisticated, self-conscious, all-round man of letters. Many American novelists can and should be read as if they were lyric poets: the critic can go straight to the central issue of sensibility, define the dominant emotion in his subject's work, seek out the manner in which emotion is related to, and maybe dominates, the technique—and come out with a reasonably trustworthy account of the novelist's meaning and worth. But such a method won't work with Warren. He is too learned. He has studied Proust, James, Gide, and Dostoevski, not to speak of worthies like Percy Lubbock, and he knows how to contrive such a degree of dramatization that it is hard to catch him attributing his own emotions to the people in his books. This ability to disappear behind his characters does not, of course, necessarily make him a better novelist, but it certainly does make him different from most of those whom we have come to think of in recent years as our best.

But Warren, for all his qualities, falls considerably short of greatness. Here is a man whose talent leaps out at the reader from every page that he writes, who truly commands the English language, who has mastered the novelist's craft, and who can create characters. And yet we come to the end of his books with a feeling that somehow we have just missed having that superlative reading experience which a genuinely superior novel provides. Why?

Surely the answer does not lie in Warren's material—the kind of people and the kind of life he writes about—for great novels have been made of material of all kinds. Nor does it lie in a simple failure of technique. I suspect, rather, that the difficulty comes from Warren's basic attitude toward his material, which forces him to put more strain on his technical ability than it can bear without giving off, at inopportune moments, a very audible creak. The test of any technique is whether or not it gives the illusion of life. Creaking dissipates this illusion.

Warren's novel—meaning now the fundamental novel which Bernard DeVoto, in *The World of Fiction*, says that every novelist writes again and again under various forms— grows out of a dynamic background provided by the clash of cultures which has plagued the South for more than a century, in which the old poverty-ridden, agrarian culture defends itself against a progressive, aggressive, basically urban one. The conflict is internecine, for even though the new culture is allied with northern and eastern money, there are southerners on both sides. Money is always involved, but so many emotional and moral stresses are also present that the cleavage is more than economic. The agrarian remnant are most often the poor and the victims of exploitation. They are also the decent, the genuine, the simple-hearted, with whom the reader's sentiment is easily enlisted.

What is at issue is quite distinct from the old theme of the disappearance of the plantations; more often than not in Warren's novels, the descendants of the plantation owners have joined forces with the new, urban culture, while the agrarians are the red-necks, the wool-caps, the ten-acres- and-a-mule people. Their plight commands the sympathy of the hero even when, as in the cases of Jack Burden and Jeremiah Beaumont, his personal interests and loyalties are oriented toward the other camp. And as the reward of his allegiance, the hero finds himself caught between several sets of millstones.

In *Night Rider* the small tobacco farmers are being

squeezed so hard by the eastern buyers that they form an association which begins as a bargaining agency and ends by dedicating itself completely to lawless terrorism, arson, and murder. Men like Perse Munn join it to defend themselves and their kind, and find eventually that they have had to sacrifice their own social integrity.

In *At Heaven's Gate* Bogan Murdoch, the central figure, subverts the best of the hill people and drives the rest off their farms into his mines and industries. His henchmen, like Jerry Calhoun and Private Porsum, discover that they can be faithful to Murdoch only at the expense of betraying their own agrarian people.

Willie Stark, in *All the King's Men,* is the champion of the red-necks, the protector of the poor men from the back parishes, the scrub farms, the sand-hill country. But to work for Willie, Jack Burden has to turn against the people of Burden's Landing and against the kind of social decency which, in spite of their alliance with the new culture, they represent.

And even *World Enough and Time,* romantic tale of the Kentucky frontier that it is, places its hero in the same uncomfortable situation. The bankrupt farmers want replevin to tide them over hard times and are virtually at war against the landowning men behind whom stand the eastern bankers. Jeremiah Beaumont casts his lot with the "replevin men," even though he has married the heiress to the remains of a good plantation and has few interests in common with the people he joins. Like Burden, like Perse Munn, like Jerry Calhoun and Private Porsum, his choice starts him on the road to misery.

For the hero is not only trapped between conflicting loyalties. When he casts his lot with the agrarians he turns out also to be accepting a criminal career. Perse Munn stays with the association when it is forced underground, commits one murder with impunity but is accused and convicted of one he does not commit, becomes a fugitive, and is at length hunted down and killed. Jeremiah Beaumont serves as the unwitting tool of the replevin men in killing his old bene-factor Cassius Fort, is jailed, takes flight, and is eventually murdered for the reward on his head. Jack Burden survives Willie Stark's disaster and is never technically outside the law, for the reason that Willie takes over and perverts the law; but it is also true that he has been able to serve Stark only at the cost of his own and the world's moral reproba-tion. He knows that he has been a criminal even though he has not been behind bars; and while he has not been a fugitive in the literal sense that the other heroes were, his hell-for-leather drive to California, when he learns that Anne Stanton has become Stark's mistress, is an enactment of the ritual of flight. Like the other heroes he is running away from the horrid consequences of his choice. Thus in *Night Rider, World Enough and Time,* and *All the King's Men,* the career of the hero follows the same almost mythic pattern: he assumes the sufferings of a group (i.e., the agrarians), descends into criminality, incurs condemnation, becomes a fugitive, and, in two or three cases, dies.

And what happens to the hero who makes the opposite choice? Well, "Bulls-Eye" Jerry Calhoun, the ex-All-American forward passer who comes from his father's farm via the state university to a vice-presidency of one of Mur-doch's banks, realizes too late that he has sold his birthright and criminally cheated those who trusted him. He, too, has a taste of jail (on suspicion of having murdered Murdoch's daughter), and ends up back on his father's farm, a dis-pirited moral ruin. Obviously there is little comfort in being the hero of a Warren novel. Whichever choice the hero makes, he is trapped.

He is also helpless. Symbolic of his general frustration

is his inability to establish a satisfactory sexual relationship. Perse Munn becomes so absorbed in the affairs of his association that he first neglects, then brutalizes his wife, who thereupon abandons him; he subsequently takes as mistress Lucille, the daughter of his friend Christian, but is unable to overcome the emotional paralysis which afflicts her. Jerry Calhoun becomes engaged to Bogan Murdoch's daughter, after she has already been his mistress, but she becomes aware of his moral nullity long even before he does and leaves him for the succession of men which includes her eventual murderer. Anne Stanton, at eighteen, senses a similar weakness in Jack Burden. His later marriage to the voluptuous Lois is an immense physical success, but such an emotional failure that in no time he is running after common prostitutes; and although at the end of the novel he has married Anne Stanton and is living with her, the union is surrounded by an unmistakable atmosphere of middle age and spent passion. It should also be noted that in all four novels the first sexual episode between hero and heroine takes place clandestinely under a parent's roof and in such circumstances that the danger of interruption is very real. The hero is thus not only unsuccessful in his sexual relationships; these also shadow forth the tragic atmosphere of betrayal, voluntary and involuntary, in which his life is lived.

For in the world where Mr. Warren's people live, treachery is the rule. Perse Munn's association is sold out to the buyers by men like Senator Tolliver, who perhaps formed it only so that they could betray it when the time was ripe. Munn in his turn betrays Christian, who is laid low by a stroke when he discovers that the man he has befriended has been sleeping with Lucille. And this happens after a more complex episode of betrayal in which Munn (who is a lawyer as well as a farmer) defends a fellow-member charged with murder and then learns that the wretch is in

fact guilty and has allowed an innocent Negro to be hanged
in his place. Jack Burden first becomes attached to Stark
when Stark learns that he has been a cat's-paw for his
original backers, and is present when at last Stark is murdered by the long-range machination of his lieutenant, Tiny
Duffy; and Burden himself succeeds in driving to suicide
the venerable—and only once venal—Judge Irwin. Jerry
Calhoun finally comes to realize that his own usefulness to
Murdoch, as vice-president of Southern Fidelity, is that he
makes a fine front for swindle. Thus while it is true that
only in *World Enough and Time* is a deftly wielded knife
the actual instrument of treachery, in all the novels a bared
and secret blade could stand as a central, basic, and essential
symbol.

We note also that in these novels of the embattled
agrarians, the pattern of betrayal is also a pattern of patri-
cide—and its reverse. In *All the King's Men* the fact is literal:
Jack Burden presents Judge Irwin with irrefutable evidence
of the judge's guilt, the old man quietly shoots himself, and
that same afternoon Burden learns from his mother that he
is really Irwin's son. In the other instances, the relationship
is the familiar one so dear to psychologists: the older man
stands to the younger in the status of a father substitute.
This is not something we merely read into the texts. Mr.
Warren's criticism shows him to be thoroughly familiar with
the literature of psychoanalysis; he can hardly be unaware
of the psychoanalytical implications of his novels. They must
be intentional. The number of such father-son relationships
in his novels is amazing. Willie Stark, for instance, is surrounded not only by parasites but also by a swarm of more
or less disabled persons (e.g., Sadie Burke, Jack Burden
himself) who need him as a staff to lean on. He is as much
in the position of the Universal Father as was the late
President Roosevelt. The people who cheer him from the

State House lawn certainly see in him much more than a
mere political advocate. Each of Mr. Warren's heroes is
involved in some such system of personal relations. Perse
Munn attaches himself to one father figure after another:
Tolliver, who betrays him; Christian, whom he betrays; and
Professor Ball, who allows him to take the blame for the
shooting which has been Ball's own handiwork. Jerry Calhoun abandons his father, whose simple, clumsy goodness
embarrasses him in comparison with the silkiness of Bogan
Murdoch. The man whom Jeremiah Beaumont lures to the
door and stabs twice, quickly, in the darkness is the same
Colonel Cassius Fort who picked him up when he was a
penniless border orphan, persuaded him to go to Bowling
Green to learn what law a man could learn in those parts,
and started him on what could have been a most excellent
career. "We have all wanted to kill our fathers," says one of
the Karamazovs. Indeed! In comparison with the life of a
Warren hero in the conflict between agrarian and urban
cultures, Dostoevski's men are mild. Warren's fathers are
just as hot after killing the sons.

Obviously the world of Warren's novels is an extremely
horrid one. It is dominated by the agrarian conflict. The
conflict forces upon the hero a choice between alternatives
either of which must bring him ill. He faces a gamut of
crime, imprisonment, reprobation, flight, and probable
destruction. He finds himself impotent and surrounded by
treachery. He also finds himself both betrayer and betrayed;
and furthermore, those whom he betrays and who betray
him are those who have turned to him in need and whom
he has needed.

But a dark and repulsive world is not necessarily the
cause of a novel's weakness—as the works of William Faulkner, with which Warren's have inevitably to be compared,
testify with great eloquence. Thus we have to look elsewhere

for the answer to our question, and it is here that a recurrent characteristic of Warren's people which has no direct and immediately visible connection with the agrarian conflict acquires a certain importance. This characteristic is that frequently they are psychological enigmas.

At Bowling Green, Jeremiah Beaumont takes a room at a Mrs. Barron's and falls in with her son Wilkie, a gay blade and replevin man who initiates Jeremiah into the political brawling of the time. He also tells Jeremiah about the misfortunes of Miss Rachel Jordan, the planter's daughter who has borne a stillborn child out of wedlock to Cassius Fort. A feeling of destiny and a strange thirst for justice draw Beaumont to the girl. He makes her marry him and forces her—we never know quite how—to set as a condition of their marriage that he kill Fort. For a while they are relatively happy and Jeremiah keeps putting off his end of the bargain. Then one day a political broadside, extremely insulting to Rachel and purportedly inspired by the enemies of replevin, reaches Beaumont's hands. He murders Fort. Beaumont is apprehended, as he knows he will be, but he is confident that he has arranged affairs so that if his friends speak only what they believe to be the truth, the crime cannot possibly be attached to him. But his friends have been corrupted and even Wilkie Barron, although with a show of reluctance, testifies damagingly. Jeremiah is found guilty and sentenced to hang.

Of all who have combined to put Jeremiah in this fix, the only one to make amends is Wilkie. One night as Rachel and Jeremiah sit in jail, masked men overpower the guards. The leader is Wilkie. He arranges an escape down river to the canebrake kingdom of a degenerate French river pirate. Here Rachel goes insane, and Jeremiah contrives to escape only to be killed for money by his guards. But before he dies, Jeremiah learns that the one cause of all his misfortune, the man who sent him to Rachel Jordan, gave him the idea of murdering Fort, issued the broadside which recalled him to his flagging purpose, and in fact engineered the whole catastrophe *was no other than this same Wilkie Barron.*

Now Beaumont has always thought of himself as a free moral agent. He has even thought of the murder as a "gratuitous act"—the expression is an anachronism, of course, but the words are there. He has also been obsessed by the idea that his life is a drama of which he is both creator and protagonist. He, Jeremiah Beaumont, will arrange his own destiny. And at the end it turns out that all along he has been the helpless puppet of this backwoods Smerdyakov!

This may not be the kind of novel Dostoevski would have written if he had taken it into his head to write a story about Daniel Boone. But at this point *World Enough and Time* begins to sound a little like the celebrated *Adventures of Lafcadio*, whose author, André Gide, was one of Dostoevski's fervent admirers. In Gide's story the hero unpleasantly pushes a casual but unattractive traveling companion off a moving train, for no other reason than that he wants to commit a perfect crime, that is, one which will show no motive of the kind that the police understand. Success would constitute proof of his own freedom of conduct. But afterward he learns that he owes his safety to a skulking character named Protos. In pushing his victim the hero loses his hat, with very recognizable initials on the sweatband, as well as one of his cuff links. When the police find the hat the initials have been snipped out of it, and Protos himself later returns the cuff link to its owner. In both Gide's story and Warren's, a character who feels himself entirely free finds that someone else has arranged his destiny for him.

Yet although the freedom of Beaumont's acts is revealed to be an illusion, Wilkie Barron's acts are presented to us as entirely gratuitous. Through what motive did he come

to his diabolical role? We do not have the least idea. Barron
remains an enigma to the end of his life. We learn that after
the close of the main story he makes a brilliant marriage,
starts on a promising political career, goes to Washington,
and there commits suicide. Remorse? The reader may think
so if he likes, but there is little in the story to point to such
a conclusion.

There used to be a time when we understood what made
the characters of a novel act as they did. Their motives were
in the open. Julien Sorel behaved like the abominable little
bounder he was because he had an ingrained, if perverted,
notion of his duty to himself. Becky Sharp expected certain
things of life and directed her conduct so as to help life
provide them. Old Goriot died in his garret because his love
for his daughters ran away with his sanity. Steinbeck's Joads
took to the highway because ignorance and cupidity had
driven them off their Oklahoma land. One can say *why* the
action took place in every case. Clarity of motive was one
of the things that made art preferable to life: these people
might be knaves and fools, but one felt a certain security in
their company because their knavery and foolishness made
sense. That kind of fiction offered us an avenue into a world
more reasonably and intelligently ordered than the one
we live in.

But not any longer! Clarity of motive is another dispelled
illusion. The new psychologists have shown us our ignorance
and taught us that if we want to understand our motives
we have to buy the comprehension. Seeing how complicated
human behavior really is, we prefer to read about the incompletely comprehensible heroes of Hawthorne, Melville,
Kafka, and Dostoevski. It is not enough that Huck Finn
should fail to understand the tumult in his own heart when
it looks as if he will have to surrender poor Jim; if Mark
Twain had known what we know about writing novels,

he would have contrived his book so that the reader would
not understand the conflict either. Then critics could have
wallowed and reveled in the murk of Huck's subconscious
and emerged finally with an explanation which would have
connected Huck's discomfort with his creator's ambivalent
feelings about the conflict between North and South. In
brief, the enigmatic hero is having his day.

Doubtless the case of Wilkie Barron should not be taken
too seriously. He appears in a "romantic" novel, and what is
romantic had better be kept thoroughly so. But it is to be
noted that Warren scatters his enigmas all over the place,
both in this book and in the earlier ones. We hardly understand the feeling of drama and destiny that drives the hero,
and Rachel Jordan's conduct can scarcely be explained by
the fact that she has had an illegitimate child. Willie Stark
is also a puzzle. No one watches Stark more closely than
Jack Burden, or knows him better; but Burden is never quite
able to decide what he thinks of his boss. At the end of the
book he has still to convince himself, if he can, that "Willie
was a great man." Now, judged by his life, Willie was a
political plug-ugly, a public plunderer, an adulterer, and a
number of other unattractive things. If he is to be taken as
great, we can only take him as such on the strength of his
motives. And since not even Burden can penetrate these
motives, we are in the presence of one real enigma and
possibly two—for Burden's motives also are somewhat in
shadow.

Bogan Murdoch's case is rather like Stark's: after his
empire has collapsed and his associates have discovered
the extent of his malefactions, there stands Murdoch, boast-
ing to the newspapermen with dignified if tarnished heroism
of how much he can still do to bring a new structure out of
the debris, pleading with the public to trust him. This man
has not been broken by the loss of his business, the alienation

of his wife, or the murder of his daughter, although he has a clear though indirect responsibility in all three events. And what explains his behavior? Inhuman callousness? Self-delusion? Hypocrisy? One explanation is as good as another in the absence of any definite indication from the author.

The same sort of mystery surrounds the character of Perse Munn; but even without his evidence it is possible to affirm that in at least three novels out of four, the motives of one or more of the leading characters are highly secret. Of the two options open to the novelist—to explain the characters by speaking in his own person, or to allow us to understand them through their action—Warren exercises neither.

An examination of one aspect of his technique suggests that he consciously intends not to exercise either option. I mean the aspect which, since Henry James, we have been calling point of view, which has to do with the kind of mediate position the author takes between the action of his novel and the reader. The manuals of fiction catalogue the various possibilities: the omniscient narrator, the non-participating observer, the first-person participant, and so forth. In the course of four novels Warren has tried four different stances.

The action of *Night Rider* is seen mostly as the central actor would have seen it, and is narrated in the third person by the novelist. But the action is seen always from a considerable distance. We are never permitted any intimacy with the hero, and are prevented from identifying our fate with his and thus forming that sympathy which is so essential. We are *told* how he feels, but we can hardly say that we *feel with* him. As a matter of fact, we never get on first-name terms with him: other characters in the story call him Perse, but in the summaries of the action, where the novelist speaks directly to the reader, he refers always to Mister

Munn. This may be only a symptom, but it is a richly suggestive one and cannot fail to have its effect on the reader:
few of us can work up much interest in the fate of a man
we know so distantly. There is a similar feeling of remoteness
in the formality of the language in which the scenes of
emotion are handled. For example, when Munn is contemplating his wife—whom he loves and will shortly lose—we
are rather chilled by such descriptive touches as: "What
light there was the woman's hair caught." And where we
should probably be given the most intensely emotional scene
of all, when Munn goes to Captain Todd's house to tell the
old man that young Benton Todd has been killed in the raid,
we get absolutely nothing at all. Such remoteness seems
to me a major defect of the book.

At Heaven's Gate, a much more complicated novel than
its predecessor, is mainly about the people who gravitate
toward Bogan Murdoch. Again the story is told by a third-
person narrator, but this time with the action seen through
the eyes of various characters according to what opportunity
offers. Meanwhile, a parallel narrative, told as a first-person
confession in chapters alternating with those of the main
action, narrates the life of a simple, virtuous hill man named
Ashby Porsum Wyndham. Wyndham fights with his brother
and leaves their farm for a woman, goes to work in Murdoch's
mine, is fired for fighting, sees his wife and child die, and
gets religion. He takes to the road, preaching salvation; is
at last jailed because one of his followers shoots a policeman;
and then, refusing to leave the jail because convicted by his
crazy conscience, he stands at the end of the book as a
symbol of simple, agrarian honesty. Here the two strands of
the novel come together. Wyndham's example inspires his
cousin Private Porsum (the local war hero) to tell the truth
and thus bring the Murdoch empire down about Murdoch's
ears. Paradoxically, the secondary story is much more of a

success than is the main one. We see and know Ashby Wyndham because we see through his eyes and know how life looks to him. But although we see Bogan Murdoch through the eyes of a variety of characters, we do not quite see what his wife hates so in him, or quite why his daughter leaves home, or how he so completely takes in young Jerry Calhoun. We are never permitted to look directly into Murdoch or to look at the action as he sees it. One man seems more clear-eyed than the rest, but he, the accountant Duckfoot Blake, is characterized as eccentric, and we never know what authority to attribute to his vision. As a result, Murdoch remains enigmatic.

A similar condition obtains in *All the King's Men*, and explains why this otherwise excellent novel is not completely successful. Jack Burden stands near the center of the story and does the narrating. We know what Burden knows about Stark, understand when he understands, are baffled when he is baffled. Unfortunately, Burden is a frequently baffled young man as well as a tortured, maladjusted one, and he never comes to see his boss plain. The political-moral ambiguity which has annoyed so many critics of *All the King's Men* rises out of this technical difficulty. If the action of this novel were seen by any eye unbeclouded by its owner's neuroses, the illusion of reality might be less intense; but the ambivalence of feelings about Willie Stark would certainly disappear without delay.

It is significant that the novel in which Warren succeeds best in handling the point of view is also the one in which—because the characters are not our contemporaries, because the issues involved are not issues which confront the ordinary reader, and because the nature of the story is frankly romantic—the enigmatic character as such is most easily acceptable. In *World Enough and Time* the story falls in the third person and the narrator, anonymous, unseen, and only occasionally felt, is a historian reconstructing from the available documents the tragedy of Jeremiah Beaumont. (The real-life Jeroboam Beauchamp left a confession which, together with the transcript of his trial, has been used by a number of writers including William Gilmore Simms, Thomas Holley Chivers, and Edgar Allan Poe.) Under the persona of the historian, for one thing, Warren is free to write as he likes. He was not free in this sense in *All the King's Men,* where the narrator had to stay in character. Jack Burden's characteristic expression was slangy, painful-ironic understatement, whereas Warren has a penchant for intense, powerful formal prose. There are places where Jack Burden, without much warning, suddenly develops a strikingly formal literary style, so that the reader gets the feeling that Burden is resting for a moment and has turned over the narrator's job to Warren. In *World Enough and Time,* on the other hand, Warren can appropriately luxuriate in his rich prose:

She stood there in her black dress, panting, in the powerful humming July afternoon. Beyond the garden where the yellow roses hung in the heat, the cornfield stretched away on one side, and the corn at that season would be waist-high, savagely green, swelling in stalk and blade from the fat soil and the sun. In the trees behind her the July flies would make their grinding, remorseless, barbaric sound like a nerve twitching in her head. From the stone gateposts the rutted red-clay lane, dusty now, fell away, leading to cabins and houses she could not see, to faces she would never know, to forests, to the wilderness itself, but not to Virginia.

One is always justifiably suspicious of critics who proclaim that certain qualities of prose can take the place of other desiderata in a novel. But one actually is swept along by the flow of words in *World Enough and Time.* It is a vast advantage to the novelist to have found a device which makes large quantities of writing like the above appropriate.

In his other books, Warren has found no such device. He has renounced his natural eloquence in order more freely to manipulate the point of view. In such a self-conscious writer who knows so well what he is about, this sacrifice clearly indicates how important it is (to him) to keep the motives of the main characters obscure.

Actually, their motives *have* to be kept secret. Just imagine for a moment that the reader of *Night Rider* had been allowed to become intimate with Perse Munn and developed a certain sympathy for him. Certainly a much more rigorous treatment of Munn's motives would have been required. For a man like old Captain Todd, represented in the book as the incarnation of integrity, does not have Munn's trouble. He joins the association and as long as it remains more or less legal and above ground he stays with it; but when it departs on its career of desperate, underground action, he withdraws, decently and with dignity, taking the respect of his fellow-members with him. His course is the course of wisdom, prudence, and morality. The first question a reasonably moral reader wants answered is: Why should not Munn have behaved in the same way instead of holding to his hell-bent course?

Warren's kind of novel *requires* an enigmatic character in its center because the frustrated, criminal, fugitive hero, moving through a world where no man including himself can be trusted, cannot be conceived as completely purposeful and completely aware of the meaning of his acts. If he were, the whole structure of his fictional world would fly apart. Ask Jack Burden to wipe his eyes and see Willie Stark clearly for the thug he is, and he will have to decide either to reject the man permanently or else accept him with overt cynicism. For him to do either, of course, would be to destroy the fiction. Thus the final burden falls upon the technique. It is a testimony to the excellence of Warren's craftsmanship that the creaking of the machinery is not more frequently audible.

In a sense Warren's trouble stems from the fact that he is a "southern regionalist." The particularly exacerbated form of regionalism which developed among southern intellectuals during the depression was as curiously unrealistic a resistance to events as American cultural history has seen in a long time. It resolutely turned its back upon the problems which confronted the country as a whole and tried to make a separate peace. Critics have tried now and then to align the mentality behind it with the varieties of extreme conservatism prevalent at the moment in Europe. The parallel does not hold, because these southerners were not, as the Europeans were, engaged in protecting economic and social privilege. Instead, they were protecting a dream.

Now dreams, heaven knows, are full of psychological significance, especially those daydreams we call fantasies. The agrarian daydream of the early thirties was just such a fantasy as a man creates when, because he is unable to cope with reality otherwise, he fashions a fiction which settles his problem effectively enough to let him go on living.

One would have to be highly unobservant not to recognize this fantasy as it appears in Warren's novels. The essential pattern of his stories repeats itself with a regularity which is almost obsessive: a young man assimilates his fortunes to those of the culture which produced him, and is destroyed by the same forces which are destroying the culture.

Agrarian regionalism as literal fact is on its way out. Fast transportation, mass production, and other such blessings are finishing it off. The radio, the movie, the syndicated editorial, the chain store, the large central factory with long lines of distribution, all conspire to kill out the differences between people of various regions. Rochester dresses us, Hollywood entertains us, Detroit flashes us around the country. What is left of the old regional differences is the psychological reality; the region is a state of mind. And the state of mind that Warren's novels reflect is a singularly unchanging one.

J. Saunders Redding, as keen an observer of the South as one could want, once told an interviewer for the *New York Times Book Review* that he deeply regretted Warren's leaving the South. I doubt whether he has anything to regret. True, Warren now eats and sleeps in the North, but his imagination has stayed behind him in his old country. The novels testify loudly that it has stayed agrarian.

Now there is nothing illegitimate about being a regionalist or an agrarian. But apparently the imagination of the artist can become so thoroughly dominated by his agrarianism that his work loses a certain actuality. We live in a world menaced by more devastating things than the disappearance of the agrarian culture, and the agrarian fantasy is remote from our concerns. To the red-necks Willie Stark may have appeared as a protector and savior—that would be his meaning to an extremist agrarian; to the rest of us, in other words to Warren's readers, Willie was a monster who threatened to destroy us. In general, the same turning away from the actual is the essential source of the weakness of Warren's novels.

He and his colleagues had earlier developed a type of literary criticism which is exposed to the same stricture. These people were some of the most gifted critics we have had. We needed badly the lesson they gave us in close reading of the texts, and their contribution includes not only the criticism they have written but also the general advance in the quality of American criticism which has come about largely through their example. But these critics went so far

in their particular direction that much effort has since had
to be spent in getting criticism back on center. The members
of the circle that grew up around John Crowe Ransom were
so devoted to literature that they attributed to it values
which transcended the values of life. Anyone who compares
the critical work of Allen Tate or of Warren with that of a
critic like Lionel Trilling, who has learned much from them
without losing his sense of actuality, must realize what a
towering advantage it is to be aware of the relations between
a book and the life of the man who reads it. The "new"
criticism lacks a certain desirable relevance.

So do Warren's novels. Had he wanted to, Henry Nash
Smith could have added to his *Virgin Land* a neat little
appendix on Warren's books as belated treatments of the
"Myth of the Yeoman." As *Virgin Land* makes clear, the
Myth of the Yeoman lost its relevance, except as a historical
item, many years ago.

There are southerners who wear the South about their
necks like the albatross. They assume all the "weaknesses"
and "faults" and "guilt" of the South that we hear so much
about. They brood and worry. There are two figures in
Warren's books who have great significance in this connection. One is Jack Burden, turning at the end of his own story
to devote his life to studying the story of Cass Mastern.
The other is the anonymous historian studying, laboring to
understand (without ever quite reaching its ultimate meaning) the story of Jeremiah Beaumont—a character who was
like Cass Mastern in many ways. They seem to me to bear a
certain resemblance to the novelist himself. They are devot-
ing themselves, as he is, to the contemplation of the unactual.

Warren will cease to be merely very good, and become
excellent, when and if he decides to get rid of the carcass
of a dead bird.

6
Erskine Caldwell

the dangers of ambiguity

THERE is a special sort of humor in America, native to our earth and deep-rooted in our history. Its material is the man who has been left behind in the rush to develop our frontiers, the man who has stayed in one place, out of and away from the main current of our developing civilization, so largely untouched by what we think of as progress that his folkways and mores seem to us, at their best, quaint and a little exotic—and, at their worst, degenerate. The canon of jokes about families who have one son in an asylum and a daughter in the reformatory and the "little feller" at Harvard—"Yeah, he's in a bottle. He's got two heads"—is enormous, frequently lurid, and invariably fascinating. Geographically, it covers the country, although the bulk of contributions seem to have come from the East: the islands off the coast of Maine, the Vermont hills, the Jackson White area along the lower Hudson, the back counties of the Allegheny Ridge states, Georgia, the swamps of Florida, and then over across to the Ozarks. It has been the main source, as well as the great strength, of Erskine Caldwell's novels.

If this seems a little strange at first, if it is difficult to square the wild and blood-chilling violence of some of Caldwell's work with his sharing in a great American humorous tradition, we have only to pick up a novel like *Georgia Boy*. In this book the elements which have now and then scandalized a good part of the reading public are for once lacking, and it is possible to see how after all the man has an impressive gift for making literary comedy out of the stuff which we most often associate with the irreverently ribald periodical press, not to say the smoking car. *Georgia Boy* is a sort of *Tobacco Road* obviously sweetened down for the carriage trade. The rampant sexuality, the murderous ignorance, the bitterly depressing picture of Georgia life which characterize Caldwell's other books are gone. What we have left is the feckless figure of Pa Stroup. He carelessly lets the family's goats get on the roof of the house; he goes into politics via the office of dogcatcher, and fills the local pound by the highly practical method of baiting the dogs with raw meat; he substitutes for the sexton and tolls the bell for a funeral when it should be pealing for a wedding; he steals a heifer by luring it away from its pasture, and carries off his neighbor's property to sell for scrap; he buys a paper-baler and gets so enthusiastic over its money-making possibilities that he throws into it not only the hymnals which have been entrusted to his wife, but even the wallpaper from the family living room. One may detect a note of seriousness in the comedy, of course. The man is presented as a small-town southerner, ignorant, lazy, too soggy-minded to be either honest or successfully dishonest, moral only because immorality requires effort, and proud at all the wrong times of all the wrong things. ("Be a good Stroup," says Pa Stroup's brother Ben as he is being taken back to the penitentiary from which he has recently escaped.)

If we like, we may see in all this a condemnation of the region which produces such fundamentally useless people. But there is no question at all about Caldwell's intention in the book, and there is no mistaking the fact that he is consciously exploiting a comic talent of considerable dimensions, and using for material one aspect of the vein just

described. *Georgia Boy,* although there is no point in claim-
ing that it is a great or even a significant book, is something
like what Mark Twain might have done had he come from
Georgia and found himself in a playful mood, and if he
had wanted to be sure of not offending his public. It is also
an important key to understanding Caldwell.

For at base most of Caldwell's books have comic implications. "Niggers will get killed," says dimwit Dude Lester
just after he has killed one with Bessie's Ford; "don't seem
to be nothing you can do about it." "I don't mind seeing a
dead darky once in a while," says Clary Horey in *Journeyman,* "but I sure do hate to see one of my hands passing
away on me at this time. It's planting time and no other.
If Hardy was to die, I'd have to get out and do some work
myself." This is pathetic stuff, in a way, and—to the delicate
conscience—bitter: certainly all the wormwood of the predicament of the underprivileged southern white is in it, all
the callousness and invincible ignorance for which circumstances are to blame. We have to achieve a certain detachment before we can laugh at it, and laughter is easier if one's
taste is not too discriminatingly genteel, and if one is not
too particularly sentimental.

The comic strain persists from book to book. There is
no doubt that fat Sheriff Jeff McCurtain in *Trouble in July*
is another version of the Jeeter Lester-Pa Stroup pattern:
gone to seed physically, shiftless, morally vague, too inert
for any sort of planned action, spineless. We recognize him
by his habitual technique for handling a crisis—he always
disappears on a fishing trip as soon as he scents trouble and
stays out of sight (much as he hates fishing) until everything
blows over. When the county judge who owns Jeff, fat body
and soul, decides that this time the law must be enforced
for reasons of political expediency, the sheriff does everything he can think of to avoid the issue. His frantic wriggling,

his terrified efforts to "keep this lynching politically clean"
and to keep himself out of danger, his persistence in blinding
himself to every sort of moral question involved, identify his
comic type. His best expedient, the product of hours of
desperate casting-about for an exit from his impasse, is to
sneak into a cell-block in his own jail under cover of darkness
and, in hopes of making it look as if he had been locked in
by the lynchers, to throw his keys out through the bars. But
he discovers with the simultaneous arrival of daylight and
his suspicious wife that he has shut himself in the same cell-
block with a comely colored girl whose presence in the jail
has already aroused his wife's jealousy!

At this point, of course, the similarity to *Georgia Boy*
ends abruptly. The comedy of *Trouble in July* goes hand in
hand with a particularly disturbing kind of violence. The
impending lynching is an especially horrid affair. That the
white girl is a dubious character with the makings of a
nymphomaniac, as one member of the lynching party testifies, makes no difference; neither does the strong chance
that the boy is in every way blameless, nor the fact that
even the unastute McCurtain can see these things. "It's not
an easy thing to say about brother whites," he remarks, "but
it has always looked to me like them folks up there never
was particular enough about the color line. However, a
nigger man ought to be more watchful, even if it is one of
those white girls up there in the sand hills." The reader
is upset by the knowledge that this black boy stands no more
chance than the other Negro stood against Dude Lester's
Ford. But what is even more upsetting is the gruesome joy
of the participants: the way so many of them make the
whole episode a social event, the pathological mass-delight
when the girl shows the crowd the great hole which the
rapist is supposed to have torn in her dress. The mob, wanting no further proof, starts the man hunt in a welter of

sexual excitement by stripping and burning with turpentine a Negro girl who has done nothing worse than fail to have the hunted boy in her cabin. The Negro boy is finally handed over to his pursuers by a man who does not believe him guilty, but who cannot face the social consequences of letting him get away. The sheriff, who has never lost hope that somehow his pitiful excuses for not taking action will seem valid, arrives on the scene to find that the lynching is over and that the girl, having confessed that she had never been raped at all, has been stoned to death by the mob in a frightening mixture of sex-lust and blood-lust.

In technique this novel, rather than the all too famous *Tobacco Road*, is Caldwell's most successful book to date. Here comedy and violence blend together and support each other. We accept Jeff McCurtain originally under the comic convention which permits the creator of a comic figure to exaggerate. Then we accept the story of the lynching because we have previously granted the existence of the character whose weakness, which we have seen as comic, is what makes the abomination of the lynching possible. We have known from the beginning that however comic Jeff may be, trouble is inevitable, and when it comes it is the more terrible because we have seen it coming so long. There is no clash between the comic mood and the horrid catastrophe into which it resolves. The effect of the book is thus powerful and unified.

The violent shock of its impact on the reader identifies *Trouble in July* as belonging to the novel of violence type, but at the same time the book stands apart from other novels of violence. When Caldwell is at his best—as I believe he is in *Trouble in July*—he reveals two special characteristics: the strangely powerful admixture of comedy and violence which he contrives, and the particular nature of the violence in which he deals. In relation to this second factor, a comparison with Steinbeck is obligatory. There is violence and to spare in Steinbeck's books, but it is violence into which the characters are forced by circumstances that are clearly, immediately visible. If the people in *The Grapes of Wrath*, for example, or *In Dubious Battle* are not violent, they will perish. If they are successful in their violence it will lead them to a better life. But Caldwell's people are frequently violent only because violence is the one available satisfaction of their depraved emotions; they torture and burn and murder for the same reasons that they writhe and howl in church; their compulsive frenzy must be assuaged through a sort of bloodletting before they are able to bear the wretchedness of their lives. There is nothing unhealthy about Steinbeck's characters; but Caldwell's are in process of degeneration, they smell of rot. Part of this is attributable to Caldwell's material; he works with life in rural Georgia, or else with rural Georgians transplanted in the towns, and he counts as one of the important group of writers who, in interpreting the region to the rest of the world, have "taken the magnolias out of the South." His material, as Caldwell interprets it, is especially rich in the comedy which we have examined, and in extraordinarily repulsive violence. The old South of bygone literary tradition was a beautiful, sometimes cloying never-never land. The present South, in the new tradition which Caldwell is helping build, is a kind of Gothic horror-chamber.

This may make it seem merely that one sort of Romanticism has been supplanted by another; but surely by this time the word Romantic must have ceased to be a term of critical reproach. It is certainly not unfair or uncomplimentary to identify Caldwell with the line of the great exponents of horror. On the basis of his juxtaposing of comedy and horror, he might even be placed in the line of contrivers of antithesis which runs back through Hugo to

Shakespeare—and there is certainly ample precedent in the "Arkansaw Difficulty" chapter of *Huckleberry Finn*. Impressive literary reputations have before now reposed on less.

But now we have to ask why it is that Caldwell's literary reputation in America is not more impressive than it is. Why is it, not that the French and Russians—to whom the appearance of a Caldwell translation is a literary event which brings staid reviewers to their feet cheering—like him so much, but that we, as a reading public, like him so much less? Why, in other words, is he a good author who has written only one completely successful book? The answer lies in his handling of violence and comedy in the rest of his output. We may take *Tragic Ground* as an example.

Taste inhibits a detailed rehearsal of the episodes of this book, not to say the quotation of certain passages which identify the comedy element with the tradition of American humor habitually exploited by Caldwell. But Spence Douthit and his family come straight out of this American folklore. Hillborn poor whites, now transplanted and stranded in an industrial slum, they are certainly below what we like to think of as the human level. Maud, the slattern wife, arises from her sickbed only when under the influence of "Dr. Munday's" richly alcoholic tonic, on which occasions she is prone to rocket about the neighborhood in the buff, or to threaten the social worker, the family's only source of help, whom she regularly mistakes for a fancy-woman with designs on Spence. Spence catches his elder daughter in his own house *flagrante delicto* with a semi-hospitalized veteran, but fails to do anything about it because of their argument that they are almost married, i.e., they have the license but no time for the ceremony. The younger daughter, Mavis, has just left home after being seduced by the next-door neighbor, against whom Spence does feel a certain resentment since "he might have let nature take its course." It is Mavis' employment in a combination road-house-brothel called The White Turkey that brings in the social worker—a type, we should note, appearing rather frequently in the back-country humor from which Caldwell draws his comedy. "You must feel free to talk to me," she counsels Spence, "because I am here to help you. You must not consider me a stranger trying to pry into your private affairs, but a sincere and trustworthy friend who wants to help your family adjust itself to the complex pattern of modern life. During cycles of economic and social readjustment, each member must co-operate as to—well, as to unity. Is that clear, Mr. Douthit?" "I can't say as it is, Miss," replies Spence. The social worker tells him that Mavis has become a prostitute within four days after leaving home. "That makes her my daughter if anything does," Spence avers somewhat proudly; "when I set out to do something, I go whole hog or nothing."

From here in the story revolves around this lady's efforts to get the Douthits out of trouble and out of town, and with Spence's valiant attempts to remain in both. He does agree to try to get Mavis out of The White Turkey ("They tell me it's a real high-class place") but the inevitable happens: he gets drunk on the money he has stolen from Maud, fails to find Mavis, and spends the night with one of the other girls.

All this should suffice to identify Spence with the other Caldwell characters we have scrutinized, but a bit more is necessary. Spence returns home the next day without Mavis, but with a curious individual named Bubber in tow. He has had the thought that Mavis, with all the things she must have learned recently, will make someone a particularly interesting wife. Bubber, whose interest in the talk about a marriageable daughter has led Spence to think of him as a prospective husband, turns out actually to be a sort of talent scout for The White Turkey. Once the pair get to Spence's house, Spence, unable to produce Mavis, strips the drunken Bubber and locks him in for safekeeping until the errant child turns up.

But enough of this. Obviously it will take a *deus ex machina* to close the story. The social worker—who, be it remembered, is our agent and society's agent—is utterly incompetent to cope with such people. Caldwell rings down the curtain by bringing back the now completely married elder daughter, who with her husband will take the family back to the hills. Maud does not want to go: Mavis has been committed to a home where it would be so nice to visit her on Sundays. And Spence is already thinking of ways to persuade his son-in-law to finance a return, one of these days, to the slums. "You just can't," he thinks, "keep digging a man up by the roots and setting him down in different parts of the country and expect him to be satisfied the rest of his life."

Thus most of *Tragic Ground*, in spite of its title, is straight comedy of the type which we have seen Caldwell consciously exploiting elsewhere. Admittedly it is comedy of people who cannot cope with life, a dreary enough picture of adult debauchery and juvenile delinquency, of drunkenness and prostitution and worse; but the whole tradition of humor to which we have attached Caldwell's comic materials is open to the same charge. So is most comedy. One could raise somewhat similar objections to *Candide;* and it would be entirely possible, by identifying ourselves with and sympathizing with Arnolphe, to make a powerful tragedy of *School for Wives. Tragic Ground* is the comic reflection of an undesirable social situation. And it would not be too unreasonable to claim that *Tragic Ground* even follows the prescription to instruct while giving pleasure—always provided, of course, that we can take pleasure from the comic

type which resorts, when reduced to lowest terms, to wondering whether now that April is here it is not appropriate
to get Gran-daddy out of the privy.

I insist on this aspect of *Tragic Ground* because one can
easily imagine how a book like this, however distasteful to
the sensitive, could pile up a really tremendous force. If
it were written entirely as straight comedy, we could probably be trusted to feel all the searing irony which arises
from the discrepancy between the ludicrous antics of the
characters and the circumstances which make them behave
as they do. We would be entirely aware that they are
unfortunate, depraved animals, and that we, as members
of a free society which resolutely persists in considering itself
enlightened, are in some measure responsible for their
depravity. Knowing that the central figure of any comedy
is in a sense a victim of the audience, we would realize that
a society which does no more about the sufferings of a
Spence Douthit than simply to laugh at them might do well
to examine its own conscience. Caldwell's book, written as
straight comedy, could have been one of those which bridge
the gap between comedy and tragedy: comedy so long as
author and reader manage to remain somewhat Olympian
and detached, but full of tragic implications as soon as the
Olympian mood should pass.

But it is not in Caldwell to let the wild comedy of *Tragic
Ground* run straight on to its own ridiculous conclusion.
Spence has a friend named Floyd who runs a scrubby store
in their slum and is surrounded by a raft of children. Unlike
Spence, he has enough brains to be unhappy. When Bubber
escapes from Spence's house without his clothes, he takes
refuge in a shack on Floyd's place, and there Spence and
Floyd catch him in the act of seducing one of Floyd's adolescent girls. Floyd murders him, briefly and messily, with
an ax. The two men then drop the body in a near-by canal,

and the story proceeds. Later Floyd takes to brooding over what is bound to happen to every family in the slum, and attempts, undetected, to burn the place down. And at the end of the story, just as Spence and his family are setting off for the hills, we learn that Floyd has given himself up to the police.

At this point the reader's task becomes a hard one. Up to now Caldwell has been enjoying the comic writer's privilege, and we have not asked him to make a literal report on life or to give us "true" people; we have allowed him to exaggerate, to pick and choose his types without reference to their being "representative," and have absolved him in advance of libel against the actual residents of the locality he chooses to write about. This was what permitted him, in *Trouble in July*, to make such effective use of Jeff McCurtain; this is what has carried us through the early part of *Tragic Ground*. But now, after Caldwell has said, "Here are my people and here is how they act, and here are certain implications which, if you can read, tell you that you have a certain responsibility for their actions," he still feels that this is not enough, and he cries: "Pretty funny, isn't it!— Now look how horrible it can be." Naturally we recoil.

And we feel somehow that we have been tricked. This game of suddenly bringing a corpse to the party destroys our confidence, to say the least. Here we have been watching a comedy—a comedy with ominous undercurrents, to be sure, but still recognizable as a comedy—and without warning Caldwell produces a violent catastrophe out of the materials which he has been treating as comic. This is true not merely of one book. Jeeter Lester's monumental shiftlessness makes episodes like the trip to town to sell the blackjack hilariously funny, but subsequently it kills him. Will, in *God's Little Acre*, is shot during the strike because of his energy, which has made him a leader—and which previously had made him the hero of a series of sexual adventures that, in spite of noteworthy ominous qualities, were part of a comic situation. They are killed by the thing which we have taken to be comic, just as Bubber has been killed as much by Spence's foolish whim to marry off Mavis as by Floyd's revolt against the doom which is closing down on his slum-rotten family. Sooner or later the reader comes almost to wonder whether he has not been wrong all the time in looking on any of Caldwell's novels as comic, and even suspects himself of a sort of guilty perverseness for having done so.

Now Caldwell is a famous reporter as well as a novelist, and has made a reputation in the field of the prose-plus-photographs documentary. And such is America that we, the public, automatically attribute special authority to the man who gives us a grim view of things as they are, especially if he does it in the weekly newspicture magazines in collaboration with a talented photographer. This special authority which we attribute to a man like Caldwell tends to undermine our confidence in our original interpretation of his work as comedy.

We have to grant, furthermore, that there are places in Caldwell's work where obviously no comedy is intended. *A House in the Uplands,* for example, is clearly an attempt to get at the sad drama of the decline of the once powerful southern families, the degeneration of the aristocracy. A kind of dark terror (not horror) presides over this story of a girl who discovers she has married a man whose blood and character have disintegrated. It is closer to Faulkner than it is to any of Caldwell's other novels, and—whatever its quality—there is no question of any comic intention. We must also grant that in *Tobacco Road,* which we have taken as comedy, there is also a vein of sermonizing in the chapters where Caldwell speaks for himself and explains

5

the course of events which has produced such people. Such considerations as these must strengthen our discomfort.

Yet if all of Caldwell's novels are taken into account, the case for documentary realism cannot stand alone for long. If it could, heaven help the sovereign state of Georgia.

Read as a documentary piece, a book like *Journeyman* becomes intolerable. Here is a traveling preacher who barges in uninvited on poor Clay Horey, looking for lodging first, and next for a woman. Even Clay doesn't like it, and Clay is another Jeeter. The first night on Clay's farm the preacher makes overtures to Clay's present wife, Dene, and before morning takes the wife of Clay's Negro field hand. Later Clay's previous wife, Lorene, turns up to see whether Clay has ever gotten around to having a doctor treat their child for the venereal disease with which they have endowed him. When the preacher learns that Lorene is now a practicing prostitute in Jacksonville, he arranges to travel with her as her pimp on the way back south. Meanwhile he has gotten Clay drunk and started a crap game in which Clay loses, in the following order, his wife's gold watch, his car, his farm, and finally his wife herself—whom he buys back, slightly damaged, for a hundred borrowed dollars. Sex relations are as tangled as any writer has contrived to entangle them since Homer: the preacher with Lorene, Dene, and the yellow girl, Sugar; Clay with Sugar, Dene, and Lorene; Dene with the Negro, Hardy, in addition to the ties already noted; and Lorene with a neighbor named Tom.

Now the preacher appears most of all as an upcountry Tartuffe, using the cloth (to which he has only a dubious title) to dupe a country clown out of all his possessions; he is a thoroughly despicable individual in every respect, and, in his readiness to do anything including murder to get what he wants, very reminiscent of figures like Faulkner's Popeye. The book ends with his Sunday services, in which he demonstrates his ability to induce in his hearers a hysterical state of religiosity, with physical manifestations obviously related to sex, which he calls "coming through." We watch with fascination this process which we assume to be as cynical and self-interested as everything else the man has done. And then, amazingly, he "comes through" himself, is so hypnotized by his own incantation that he fails to take a collection and, instead of going off on the projected trip with Lorene, disappears without warning during the night.

One of the quotations which I brought up at the beginning to identify Caldwell's comedy with a familiar folk-humor is from this book, and it would be possible to make a case for the interpretation of the whole thing as comedy of Caldwell's characteristic type. But again the reader would be disconcerted by the sudden revelation about the preacher, and return to doubting the validity of his interpretations. Yet, on the other hand, to take the tale as literal reporting is almost insuperably difficult. There is, of course, the terrible possibility that much of this stuff is literally true; but the fact that the exaggeration is so palpable defeats the purpose of realistic reporting in the documentary manner. Even if we were predisposed to accept the literal-reporting theory in view of the generally leftist tendency of Caldwell's politics, the whole point of such reporting, in the purview of leftist politics, would be that such things are typical of at least a considerable segment of the population of our country. The merest suspicion of comedy, of comic exaggeration, or of anything of the sort would frustrate the political purpose, and leave us exactly where we were before. In other words, to interpret Caldwell's work as reporting of this kind leaves out too much.

This will not do. If there is an element of reporting in Caldwell's novels, it is of another and less satisfactory sort. Caldwell has always been an inveterate collector of grotesques: in *Tobacco Road* the grandmother, consumed by pellagra until she is a dehumanized hag; Bessie, with no nose; the girl with the harelip, so hideous no male can keep his eye on her; Jeeter himself, a sort of he-witch. In *God's Little Acre* Pluto is so fat he can hardly move about; in *Trouble in July* Sheriff Jeff McCurtain has so big a belly his wife has to lace his shoes. Bubber, the repulsive character in *Tragic Ground,* has a grin permanently built into his face. And these are only show cases. Behind them is a procession of women like Maud, and energy-drained, worm-eaten men like Spence. These are presented by Caldwell as people. They are also, in a sense, gargoyles. We are never sure that they are not in the stories simply because they are picturesque. There is really no good reason why Jeff and Pluto have to be incapacitated by fat, so far as the stories go. A missing nose and a harelip are not essential to *Tobacco Road,* except that they serve to make the men who can contrive to put up with them seem extraordinarily desperate for feminine companionship—in fact, picturesquely so.

In connection with this we remember that Caldwell has been general editor of a series of books on American Folkways. And what, as Professor Howard Mumford Jones once asked in a review, is a "folkway"? Of course, it has something to do with being native to a rural place, and characteristic of the people there. Yet although you and I are folk—save for the evil chance which occasionally coops us up in cities —our characteristic manners are not folkways in Caldwell's sense, and neither are the characteristic manners, which Professor Jones cites, of his youth on a midwestern farm. To be folkways, they must also be picturesque.

To get back now to Caldwell's novels: may they not also be interpreted as a sort of preliminary exploration of certain American folkways? Are they not, as much as anything else, an exploitation of the picturesque? I would hesitate to affirm that they are, but the suspicion exists and must be recognized. Not only may these people be gargoyles, inserted for their ornamentative horribleness, but their conduct may be the conduct of gargoyles; we may be watching both grotesque types and grotesque—intentionally grotesque—human activity.

Now nobody objects to looking at gargoyles, so long as we know what we are looking at. But the identification of these characters as such should, it seems to me, pretty well cancel out the possibility of reading Caldwell's novels as straight socially-conscious documentaries, and also cancel out the value of the books as serious comedy.

By itself, then, the theory that Caldwell is doing some sort of reporting is a completely inadequate basis for the interpretation of his work.

There is, to sum it all up, no completely satisfactory attitude for the reader to assume toward these books. When we read them as comedies, Caldwell carefully and disconcertingly knocks the props from under the comic element; we look then for serious, socially-conscious reporting, and the comic element spoils our view; we resort, unwillingly, to taking them as exhibits of the picturesque, only to realize that Caldwell deserves more from his reader. So we come finally to the conclusion—for which we have been searching all along—that Caldwell's novels suffer from a multiplicity of meanings which are incompatible with one another. This is another way of saying that Caldwell's own attitude toward his materials is ambiguous.

Sometimes it is childish to object to ambiguity. Ambiguity, we are persuaded, is life. And we all love *Hamlet*. Yet we hate to renounce unnecessarily that part of the human heritage which is our ingrained reluctance to admit that it is impossible to make the world conform to the logic we have invented. We demand that if we must finally surrender to ambiguity we be given something in return; we ask that the ambiguity somehow enrich us, that the meanings of a book be somehow complementary to each other, that there be layers of meaning rather than a number of conflicting meanings on the same level. The ambiguity which we are willing to accept is in the finished work, then, but not in the author's own attitude toward his material.

The French, those archenemies of the ambiguous, have read Caldwell as an exponent of the new *roman noir* and do not complain of his ambiguity. They have the additional advantage of being more remote from the material. They can read *God's Little Acre* without feeling that Pluto is always treated as a picturesque, stock character; that old Ty-Ty's frequent redesignation of the plot of ground reserved for the Almighty's benefit comes from a familiar comic tradition; that much of the farming scene is straight documentary stuff; that the fiercely animal sexuality of some of the characters, not to mention the bloodshed, has less to do with the rest of the material than with our present novelistic conventions. Nor are they, as we are, in the position of emotional involvement where Caldwell's material is concerned.

The emotional question is one to which I have not dared to give much importance up to this point, because amateur psychology is a treacherous thing. But the key to the whole discussion may be contained in it. Can it not be that Caldwell's own emotions toward his characters are somewhat unsteady? These are his people; it would be odd indeed if he did not feel strongly about them. "I would willingly trade ten thousand of those [readers]," he writes in his Foreword to *God's Little Acre*, "for a hundred readers among the boys and girls with whom I walked barefooted to school and with whom I sweated through the summer nights in the mills of Georgia." This sounds like emotional involvement. And no one, certainly, would blame Caldwell for it. But unless carefully controlled, it could show up in his writing as a sort of sentimentality. Sentimentality toward material like Caldwell's could, in turn, result in the ambiguity which bothers us. I believe—though I propose it as a suggestion only—that this is true in Caldwell's case.

Yet despite all the difficulties we have noted, Caldwell's novels have their place with those of Hemingway, Faulkner, and Steinbeck; and one of them, *Trouble in July,* is a really superior piece. His mixture of comedy and violence, when it works well, is a significant contribution to the novel of violence. Some of his creations have become part of our folklore: people who have never read a line of Caldwell know all about Jeeter Lester, and apply to the form of degeneracy to which it is appropriate the slur, "tobacco-road." After all, the only justification for spending as much time on the question of his ambiguity as we have spent here is that the ambiguity has probably frustrated the fuller development of a truly remarkable talent.

7

John Steinbeck

the utility of wrath

WE have been right all along in suspecting that there is really more than one Steinbeck. There is the Steinbeck of *The Grapes of Wrath,* of *In Dubious Battle,* and of a number of short stories, an angry man whose anger has put a real tension in his work; there is Steinbeck the extremely gifted humorist; and there is also the Steinbeck who seems at times to be only a distant relative of the first one, the warm-hearted and amused author of *Tortilla Flat, Cannery Row, The Wayward Bus, The Pearl,* capable of short stretches of some really dazzling stuff but, over the length of the book, increasingly soft and often downright mushy. In other words, Steinbeck has achieved his success by working within limi-tations which are perhaps self-imposed but which seem on the whole to be imposed on him by his temperament. They tie him down to an exclusive preference for one type of character, which recurs with surprising consistency through-out his work, and to a maximum of two emotional attitudes, one compounded of some delight and much compassion toward the people he writes about, the other of compassion and wrath.

In *Cannery Row* and *Tortilla Flat* Steinbeck's people have no commitments to society and no inhibitions worth men-tioning. They get drunk, and fight, and afterward their kindliness and native innocence make them extremely sorry

if they have hurt someone or burned a house or done anything else to be ashamed of. They have an admirable talent
for taking life exactly as it comes, with a cheerfulness which
is the virtue of the uncorrupted. None is truly vicious. The
girls in the brothel are golden-hearted business women.
Despite some tendency to fleece his customers, the old Chinese who runs the store is essentially a sweet philosopher and
as such is resigned to the certainty that many of his patrons
will default their accounts. The Mexican boys steal beans
by the ton to aid the lady who just can't help having babies,
and share their hovel with a roofless unknown whose sick
child needs a place to die. Even the biologist Doc, whose
education and investment in his laboratory obligate him
somewhat toward society, excels the first-century Christians
in sweet forgiveness when the boys throw a party for him
in his absence and ruin the laboratory doing it.

Simple, goodhearted people are so much Steinbeck's spe-
cialty that really despicable ones are hard to find in any of
his books, and it may eventually be said of him that his
greatest weakness was his inability to depict a full-length
heel, a thorough out-and-out louse. Even the German officers
in *The Moon Is Down*, against Steinbeck's manifest intention in the case of Captain Loft, have enough of this native
simplicity and decency about them to make us wish we
could forgive their iniquity. His most unsympathetic characters are women, like Curley's wife, in *Of Mice and Men*,
and the lady who was willing to sacrifice so much to have
a garden, in "The White Quail."

It is not clear how much Spanish literature Steinbeck has
read; but if he is not familiar with the old picaresque novel
he has reinvented it. His people are probably at their best
—their most characteristic—in the books wherein they are
perfectly free to be rogues in the Spanish fashion, living by
their wits, unconcerned with the moral niceties, capable

both of debauched brutality and of great tenderness. Steinbeck lacks in these books, however, the occasional intense bitterness of such stories as *Lazarillo de Tormes;* and if he intends any social criticism in books like *Cannery Row* and *Tortilla Flat,* he is even more oblique about it than the Spaniards, who had to be indirect or burn. But the lack of bitterness and the disappearance of social consciousness do not keep Steinbeck's men from being *pícaros;* they merely become *pícaros* more after the fashion of Sancho Panza, that "inevitable belly." Cervantes, like Steinbeck, was a sentimental man.

Sentimental Steinbeck certainly is, and in his more serious books this is his great weakness. But for his sentimentality he might have seen the predicament of the Okies as in some part the result of their own greed and stupidity. To the extent that we expect fiction to present a balanced and equitable report on the conditions in which Americans live —and this is something we have every right to expect when the fiction presents itself as documentary—sentimentality impedes Steinbeck's performance. There is danger in having too much compassion. His heart goes out to people who are so uncomplicated themselves that they are unable to cope with any but the very simplest ideas, and who know they suffer but have trouble knowing why. It is true that there are times when such bafflement may be an actual advantage to a book, as it is in *The Grapes of Wrath,* in which the analysis of what bothers the Joads is also a stiff problem to the reader; but in general, if the reader once feels that a character in a novel has to be wilfully dumb not to know why he is in discomfort, his pleasure gives way to irritation. Hemingway, who has always had the same trouble—as did Sherwood Anderson before him—traps himself completely in the unhappy botch called *To Have and Have Not.* We know too well that nothing is inevitable in Harry Morgan's predicament except Morgan's own wordy but fundamentally inarticulate stupidity; when Morgan has to think, he ties himself in such knots that he seems to resort to violence merely as an escape from thought. Hemingway's failure here comes from substituting compassion for brains too completely.

Because of this same tendency in Steinbeck there is something worrisome in his great predilection for half-wits and the singular beatitude which he attributes generally to the poor in spirit. There are a good half-dozen half-wits in his works, such as the unforgettable Lennie with his great homicidal gentleness, Johnny Bear with his frightening gift for mimicking what he does not understand, the twelve-year-old who tries to steal a gift for Doc in *Cannery Row*, the Mexican child digging in the orchard for the elves. On the other hand, Steinbeck's interest in this simple-mindedness is what makes him write so beautifully about boys. A boy, as far as experience is concerned, is by nature in the predicament of the half-wit: he is continually confronted by something new, different, wonderful, and beyond his understanding. In his bewilderment he is an object of compassion. This same sympathy which produces Steinbeck's half-wits also gives us "The Red Pony."

Steinbeck's zealous attention to half-wits and boys and dock-side loafers and *paisanos* and bindle stiffs has been diagnosed as a preoccupation with primitives. Let us not challenge this diagnosis as far as half-wits and boys are concerned—but if the rest are primitives, the word seriously needs definition. Society, not nature, has made them what they are. In *Cannery Row* and *Tortilla Flat* they are irresponsible and happy and inconsequential because the economic environment and the benign California climate enable them to meet their needs without serious effort or strain. Let these conditions change, let Steinbeck cease being playful, and we see another side of the people he loves. They are beyond the protection of the law, since they have no property and what they can earn is never more than they need to eat. They are the dispossessed or the unpossessing. The law which exists to protect possessions also guarantees the integrity of the one thing they have, the right to struggle for existence; but by one of the ambiguities which plague our time, the struggle for existence is more than likely to endanger the possessions of others, and the law is therewith turned against itself. When you have nothing you are very likely to move in on the holdings of the man who has something. Moreover, the man who has nothing has neither the time, the training, nor—if he comes from a line of have-nots—the brains to reason with detachment about his predicament. Either he is right or he is wrong. His empty belly tells him he is right, and he can enforce his point of view only by the violence of physical conflict. As a character he will provide action.

Take the people of *Cannery Row* or *Tortilla Flat* out of the pleasant climate and let the economic environment squeeze instead of tolerate them, and they will be out with the migrants on Highway 66 and the name of your book will be *The Grapes of Wrath*. Or simply leave them in California and turn the economic setup against them until they become desperate and angry, and you have a strike on your hands and the name of your book is *In Dubious Battle*.

If anyone else had written *Cannery Row*, the consensus of the critics might have been that this book was pretty good stuff. Of Steinbeck we expected more, and in our disappointment that he had chosen to follow his "serious" novels with a book which in some ways repeats the formula of *Tortilla Flat*, we missed the obvious fact that here better than anywhere else the source of his great power and also of his weakness was revealed: the fact that the people of

The Grapes of Wrath and *In Dubious Battle* are essentially
the people of *Tortilla Flat* and *Cannery Row*.

In *The Grapes of Wrath* these good, kindhearted, ignor-
antly immoral irresponsibles become the figures of a tragedy.
When they pull up stakes for the long drag from Oklahoma
to California, they are pushed on by a force which they
understand no better than the Greeks understood fate. We
speak of Economic Drives as the Greeks spoke of Gods, but
we know only vaguely what urges them along, and the
Joads know less than we. We know further that whatever the
Joads do they will never be able to escape, and that the
little wisps of hope they carry with them, feeble as they
are, are unjustified: disaster lies ahead; they hasten to it;
they could not turn back if they would.

Their progress hardly stops for the basic processes of life
and death. When the old grandfather dies they hurry his
body into the ground so that they can be on the way in the
morning. The grandmother dies on the truck itself while,
during her agony, Rose of Sharon and her husband have their
way with each other, sprawled on top of the load; the
beginning and the end of life alike are unable to delay the
course of the tragedy. And meanwhile at the other end of
the journey the antagonist is ready. He is animated by the
same forces that are driving the Joads, and is no more able
to let go what he has than they are to refrain from trying
to take it away from him. He is as ignorant as they of what
makes them all behave as they do. Finally in the fields and
groves of California they come to grips and both sides are
defeated, the men of Oklahoma first and within the scope
of the book; the people of California later but just as inevitably, as we who are reading realize.

We are left with no feeling that the violence of the novel
is an arbitrary thing, put there because to the author violence is beautiful or fascinatingly ugly. Because of the

inevitability of the clash, the book has the form of tragedy: like tragedy it points all in one direction; the force is so strong, the flow and sweep of the thing so inescapable, that whatever digression is in it appears as no more than a minor fault and does not obscure the novelist's purpose.

The word "form" as applied to novels is a metaphor, and a different metaphor may make this point clearer: let us say "progression." *The Grapes of Wrath* has the progression of tragedy so completely that the interpolated chapters, which explain events to the reader and which we may think of as choruses, are swept along without deflecting the tragic impetus. This is fortunate, because the book is also a road-novel. The road-novel is a favorite storytelling device to get unity running through a set of adventures which would otherwise bear small relation to one another. Conversely, the frame of the road-novel is an open invitation to episodic writing—the characters are here and something happens, they move to another place and something else happens, etc. When you can remember individual episodes in a novel better than you remember the total effect of the book, the chances are that you have been reading a road-novel, something like *Don Quixote* or *Tom Jones* or *The Sun Also Rises*, to name only great ones.

The tendency of the road-novel to break up into episodes is all the more dangerous to a novelist who tends by nature to write episodically, as does Steinbeck. He can persuade himself that he has put unity into his work where no one else sees it. There is supposed to be an interior continuity to *Tortilla Flat*, based upon the Arthurian legend and more specifically on Malory. The critics missed it unanimously. As a matter of fact, Steinbeck is the only person I have ever heard of who affirmed that the unity was there.

To achieve unity, flow, progression, men like Steinbeck and Faulkner and Hemingway are forced to be particularly attentive. Faulkner solves the problem successfully in *As I Lay Dying* by creating an atmosphere of horror which constantly mounts as the episodes progress and constitutes the primary residual effect on the reader as he finishes the book. Hemingway is completely defeated by the same problem in *To Have and Have Not*. His attempt to unite two separate episodes from the life and death of Harry Morgan, by throwing in sketches intended to show the cheap emptiness of the rich people with whom Morgan is meant to be a bitter contrast, eventuates in a book which has no more unity than a sandwich. That the same problem of unity did not trap Steinbeck testifies to the inner strength of the tragedy he conceived. I have no desire to make Steinbeck into a rather strained-looking Greek, but it seems to me that he has put into *The Grapes of Wrath* most of the elements of tragedy: the driving forces, the swift rush of events, inevitability, mounting pity and terror, clash, violence. His characters react properly in the face of evil, and the foolish things they do are pieces of eternally human foolishness.

There is a price to pay, however, for the tragedy we get. Steinbeck's compassion leads to oversimplification, a distaste for complication which extends beyond a mere dislike of complicating personalities. For our purposes it is unimportant that the original popularity of *The Grapes of Wrath* was a product of its timeliness and topical interest, that it appeared at a moment when interest in alleviating the lot of the migrants was widespread; the book is no whit greater because, as a reform tract, it did have a practical and beneficial effect on the condition of the Okies and Arkies in California. We do not now read *The Grapes of Wrath* for these reasons. The important thing for us here and now is that the plight of these people raised in Steinbeck the passion and anger which caused him to write the book. In his wrath he goes too far. He can see only two kinds of people, those like the Joads and those who whirl past the migrants on Highway 66 in expensive cars. One page of *The Grapes of Wrath* reveals the violence of the antithesis:

Languid, heat-raddled ladies, small nucleuses about whom revolve a thousand accouterments: creams, ointments to grease themselves, coloring matter in phials—black, pink, red, white, green, silver—to change the color of hair, eyes, lips, nails, brows, lashes, lids. Oils, seeds, and pills to make the bowels move. A bag of bottles, syringes, pills, powders, fluids, jellies to make their sexual intercourse safe, odorless and unproductive. And this apart from clothes. What a hell of a nuisance! . . . Beside them, little pot-bellied men in light suits and panama hats; clean, pink men with puzzled, worried eyes, with restless eyes. Worried because formulas do not work out; hungry for security and yet sensing its disappearance from the earth. In their lapels the insignia of lodges and service clubs, places where they can go and, by a weight of numbers of little worried men, reassure themselves that business is noble and not the curious ritualized thievery they know it is; that business men are intelligent in spite of the records of their stupidity; that they are kind and charitable in spite of the principles of sound business; that their lives are rich instead of the thin tiresome routines they know; and that a time is coming when they will not be afraid any more.

Over against such people Steinbeck sets the honest, jovial vulgarity of men like the transport truck drivers. You must, he implies, be one kind or the other. There is an exclusiveness here that suggests a sort of inverted snobbery; it would seem that one can't qualify as a decent individual unless one can simplify his personality to the point of sharing the ideal expressed by George in *Of Mice and Men:* "When the end of the month come I could take my fifty bucks and go into town and get whatever I want. Why, I could stay in a cat house all night. I could eat any place I want, hotel or any place, and order any damn thing I could think of. An' I could do all that every damn month. Get a gallon of whiskey, or set in a pool room and play cards or shoot pool."

This oversimplification is a pity, not because it spoils
The Grapes of Wrath (it does not), but because it prevented
Steinbeck's writing a book which would have been much
more universally American. When the Joads arrive in California and the inevitable clash arises, we see its effect only
on one party. We do not get the story of the little people
on the other side. Yet the men who fought against the Joads
were just as terrified and in the long run just as luckless.
When circumstances turn them against their own kind, the
plight of the have-a-littles is just as pitiable as that of the
have-nots. Steinbeck goes to some lengths to establish our
faith in the fact that his people are typically American, not
only by introducing the classical rural jokes about sex in the
barnyard, but by laboring over the native mysticism of Tom
and more especially of Casy, the ex-preacher who can't feel
religious without wanting a woman, too. (The mysticism is
something many of us could get along without, not because
we don't like Walt Whitman but because when we want
him we know where to get him in the original.) *The Grapes
of Wrath* would be symbolically American if the reader had
to sympathize with both sides at once, a situation familiar
to almost every American of Steinbeck's time. Some of Steinbeck's literary tragedy would have been spoiled in the
process, but we would have been thrown face to face with
the tragic ambivalence of our lives.

In this sense Steinbeck cannot be said to have made the
most of the available materials. But it is quite clear what
he has done with those he has chosen to use. For the premise
of the older novel, that nature never concludes, he has
substituted the artistic device of putting people in situations
from which they may emerge, if at all, only through bloodshed, injury, or sudden death. Such a novel *has* to conclude,
in short order, and bloodily. Whereas the reader's mood on

putting down the erosion-novel, as practiced by Wolfe and Dos Passos, is likely to be one of lyric nostalgia, he feels at the end of one of our novels of destiny, if it is any good, as if he had just finished the *Agamemnon*—that horrid tale of a hatchet murder in a bathtub.

It is no accident that the novel of violence as a type has stepped from under the auspices of the middle class, for the middle class is nonviolent by nature and does not offer proper material. Our stability abhors violence. Our relative leisure and the slowness with which our fortunes change make us apt material for the novel which studies the working of time; our relations with one another are likely to produce characters for the portrait-novel; but it is only when a member of the middle class revolts against the basic class patterns that he becomes a subject for the novel of violence. It is significant that the novel of violence (both as serious literature and in the insidious form of the whodunit) prospered most after the slump of 1929, during a period in which the class structure of the country crystallized and class differentiations became apparent.

Yet Steinbeck's exclusiveness in the choice of characters and the restricted range of his emotional attitude toward them are at times a definite advantage. The same things that made him a natural to write *Cannery Row* made him a natural to write *The Grapes of Wrath*. They also qualified him to write about a strike as no one else has written about a strike, to my knowledge, since Zola's *Germinal*.

A strike is material for literature, by definition, only when it involves suffering and violence: when it is just one of the rituals which accompany the consummation of certain economic relationships it is without literary significance. As a source of suffering and violence, meanwhile, it involves two pitfalls for the writer. One is that the individual participant sees very little of what is going on, so that panoramic treat-

ments are likely to ring false; the other, that where there is
so much violence the writer may litter his stage with too
many insignificant corpses, like the less successful Eliza-
bethans. To exploit the natural tensions of a strike without
losing the reader in details or numbing him with brutality
takes doing.

In Dubious Battle brings it off. It is not so powerful a
book as *The Grapes of Wrath,* because the outcome 'of the
fable is arbitrary. We know from the start that the strike
itself must and will fail, but the central character, Jim
Nolan, dies for reasons which may be compellingly valid
for him but do not necessarily compel us as we read. That
he should die where he does, and at that time, is the result
of his own choice. We have to take the story, then, not as
a tragedy but as a tale of latter-day martyrdom.

Jim is one of Steinbeck's ordinary, goodhearted lads who
could appropriately be off chasing frogs and getting drunk
with the boys in *Cannery Row,* but he has been caught in
the squeeze of his economic environment. His family has
been knocked to pieces in the struggle to stay alive and he
is sore enough to want to hit back. The fruit pickers' strike
which he helps organize is to be his initiation in the techniques of the active radical. He is not sure that he will be
any good at it; the thing represents to him mostly a way of
life that he wants to try. But by the time the strike is under
way, as he tells his partner and mentor, Mac, "this thing is
singing all over" him. The discouraging knowledge that the
opposition is too strong for this strike soon becomes meaningless to him; the fight must be carried as far as possible,
for its effect on all future strikes. As Jim develops and the
strike fills his whole soul, he becomes the moving power in
the battle. "I'm stronger than you," he tells Mac. "I'm
stronger than anything in the world because I'm going in
a straight line. You and all the rest have to think of women

and tobacco and liquor and keeping warm and fed.... I wanted to be used. Now I'll use you, Mac. I'll use myself and you." By the end of the book his self-subordinating single-mindedness has become a sort of radical sainthood. And as a holy man who has attained true saintliness is ready for death, so Jim is ready to die.

There is violence to spare in this book. Men are shot in cold blood. Other men are pounded to pieces. There are three cases of arson and one of mayhem and innumerable ones of bodily assault. At one point we stand by with Jim and watch Mac make jelly of the face of a teen-age boy, accepting the thing as necessary because, in terms of the strike, we know that what this lad has done must not be allowed to happen again:

"I want a billboard," said Mac, "not a corpse. All right, kid. I guess you're for it." The boy tried to retreat. He bent down, trying to cower. Mac took him firmly by the shoulder. His right fist worked in quick, short hammer blows, one after another. The nose cracked flat, the other eye closed, and dark bruises formed on the cheeks. The boy jerked about wildly to escape the short, precise strokes ...

If such a spectacle is tolerable to the reader it is because there is a sort of orderliness in all the violence in the book. The development of the strike forms the frame of *In Dubious Battle* just as progress along the road forms the frame of *The Grapes of Wrath*, and the development of the strike requires violence. Once Jim and Mac have worked themselves into the confidence of the strikers, they have the problem of directing a force of inexperienced and undisciplined men, so unschooled for the job that they must continually see violence done in order to have the stomach to do it themselves. If such men are not worked on through their brute instincts, they may at any moment lose heart and sneak away. Thus Jim and Mac have to use everything that will stir the mob. Their little friend Joy is too punch-drunk to be useful because he has fought too often with the police; when he is shot down, they put on a public funeral and exhibit his body for its effect on the mob. Ultimately they all know they are beaten. Jim, who has been shot through the shoulder, is desperate lest his men disperse without one last attempt; he wants to tear the bandages off and start his wound bleeding again so that his followers can once more have the sight of blood. This represents the perfection of Jim's soul in the way of violence. At the very end of the book he has his apotheosis. After Jim's face has been completely blown away by the blast of a shotgun, Mac brings his body back into camp and sets it up in front of the crowd in the hope of moving them to an additional violent act, screaming at them the same words he had used over the body of punch-drunk little Joy: "This guy didn't want nothing for himself . . ."

The device is obvious. Steinbeck is not an artist who hides his devices, anyway. And the device is the making of the novel. The orderliness of the violence comes from its absolute double necessity—double in that it is necessary both to the strike and to the growth of Jim's soul. This book has been misjudged by the critics, or rather has gone unjudged, because it involved so many pressing political and social problems that it was generally read as a radical tract rather than as a novel. Such a failure in insight was to be expected; the pre-atomic decade which produced the novel was not one to produce detachment in critics. Nor, perhaps, one to produce detachment in novelists either. *In Dubious Battle* is a triumph of a novelist who refuses to detach himself from his characters.

The Moon Is Down falls far short of the previous novels. It was written at a moment when Steinbeck could not well exploit his favorite themes. He was a party to the suspension, by common consent, of the struggle between the haves and the have-nots. As he reported in *Bombs Away,* his propaganda piece about the Army Air Force: "Our arguments and disunity might have kept us ineffective or only partly effective until it was too late. But Germany and Japan were bound to blunder sooner or later, and blunder they did. In attacking us they destroyed their greatest ally, our sluggishness, our selfishness and disunity." Furthermore, his favorite characters were either already in the services or else, presumably, so situated in industry as to obviate the immediate need for compassion; in either case they would not be material for a timely book, and while I have argued that Steinbeck's sense of timing does not make him good, it is also true that his best books have used timely material. He was thus forced to make a new sort of character and a new sort of story.

The story he made should be all the answer needed to the criticism that Steinbeck owes his success to the pressing topical interest of his books. *The Moon Is Down* had great topical actuality, but it did not and does not compel the interest and sympathy of the reader.

Is not this because Steinbeck's interest in his characters, and sympathy for them, are so patently theoretical here? They do not enlist his compassion. These are not the people that Steinbeck loves so much that he is indignant at their being pushed around, but rather people he feels he ought to love because he is opposed to the pushing around of human beings in general. Nothing less than a major war could have aroused Steinbeck to write about a character like the Mayor of the occupied Norwegian town. Here, as nowhere else in his work, we are aware of the great discrepancy between the skill expended and the results obtained. *The Moon Is Down* is slick as novels written for Hollywood are slick. We recog-

nize the careful performance of a professional because he
leaves us so free and undistracted by the movements of any
living characters.

The point need not be labored. It is enough to put beside
the Mayor's exit speech from *The Moon Is Down* Tom Joad's
final speech to his mother, in *The Grapes of Wrath*. It will
be remembered that the Mayor goes out to be shot after
quoting the words of the *Phaedo* which have to do with the
paying of Socrates' debt of a cock to Asclepius. Now hear
this:

"Then it don' matter. Then I'll be all aroun' in the dark. I'll be
ever'where—wherever you look. Wherever they's a fight so hungry
people can eat, I'll be there. Wherever they's a cop beatin' up a
guy, I'll be there. If Casy knowed, why, I'll be in the way guys
yell when they're mad an'—I'll be in the way kids laugh when
they're hungry an' they know supper's ready. An' when our folks
eat the stuff they raise an' live in the houses they build—why,
I'll be there. . . ."

Tom's goodbye to his mother has in it some of the home-
grown mysticism which I find annoying wherever it turns
up in Steinbeck, but there is no getting around the fact
that it also has an emotional tension to which the reader's
emotions respond; there is warmth in these words. There
is no warmth in the Mayor, nor, as he stands in print, is there
breath. Steinbeck is simply too detached from him; he and
his character are on the same side against a common enemy,
but if the Mayor did not happen to be head of a town taken
over by the Nazis it is inconceivable that Steinbeck would
even speak to him on the street. The difference between Tom
Joad and the Mayor is that Steinbeck loves Tom Joad.

But it has become increasingly apparent since the end of
the war that love is decidedly not enough. Wrath is clearly
necessary also. There is not the least shadow of doubt that
Steinbeck is extremely fond of the characters in *The Way-*

ward Bus (meaning the "good" ones, not people like Mr. and Mrs. Pritchard) and in *The Pearl*. They are his people: Juan Chicoy, for example, is a Steinbeck *paisano* with a flair for getting the best from old machinery. Compared with his passenger, Pritchard, he is honest, clean, and somehow noble —all because of his essential, overwhelming simplicity. The role of the Pritchards, husband and wife, of course repeats the role of the "heat-raddled" wealthy people who whirl past people like the Joads in *The Grapes of Wrath*. But now the antithesis seems to lack tension. And like Chicoy's bus, the story itself gets nowhere.

Besides love, Steinbeck needs wrath—an emotion strong enough to hold his pages together. And this is exactly what is lacking in his postwar books. He merely loves the people he loves and wants them to be happy. Happiness, in such a context, seems to be little more than freedom from serious worry and the uninhibited assuagement of the more pressing biological urges. It seems to reside, very largely, in the region of the pelvis. An older generation, at this point, would have talked of a fundamental lack of moral seriousness.

With the exception of Faulkner, the novelists with whom Steinbeck is inevitably to be compared seem to have written their best work under the impulse of some driving emotion. Wolfe had his intense feeling of being homeless and wronged by a country which should have provided him a home, a "door." Dos Passos, more versatile in his indignation, had his hatred of the Army in *Three Soldiers*, his great concern over what was happening to America in the *U.S.A.* trilogy; and it is rapidly becoming a critical commonplace that the inferiority of the Spotswood trilogy to the earlier work has its source in the fact that he was "puzzled"—that his emotional attitude toward his material was unclarified and indecisive; on his way to political conservatism, and to the acceptance of the status quo, he left his novelistic equipment behind him. Hemingway is at his best in books infused with vast despair, dislike of war, or militant indignation against fascism. Unless the writer can become a Faulkner and possess an imagination so thoroughly adequate that this kind of emotion is not necessary, some such compulsion seems to be requisite.

Steinbeck's writing of the fifties has nothing, however, to suggest that he will ever again be anything but a man of great, of almost overwhelming, peace. *East of Eden* is the most ambitious, in size, of all his stories, but in no way threatens to displace *In Dubious Battle* or *The Grapes of Wrath*. As always when Steinbeck is not at his best, the people are exhibits, cases, specimens. It is not hard to believe that women like Cathy exist or that they burn home and parents, commit adultery with their brothers-in-law, and retire from family life to resume the oldest of professions; but it is extremely difficult to make a woman like Cathy take on the kind of actual existence which could make her believable as a central character in a novel — especially when, as is the case in *East of Eden,* such a woman is seen entirely from the outside and the reader has no clear notion of the reasons for her behaving as she does. This is another example of Steinbeck's inability to animate really bad, or even unpleasant, people.

East of Eden is also an example of the inadequacy of Steinbeck's tolerant interest in people to provide the kind of driving force which moves the action along. The work seems to fall apart, into its component pieces. Steinbeck's favorite vehicle, one suspects, is the sketch or the short chapter, which can be joined with others to make up a book. One also suspects that his commitment to the individual subjects of these units dominates his interest and commitment to the novel as a whole. At times it is not even clear that a given sketch was in fact written for *this* particular book at all. For example, the chapter in which, toward the end of *East of Eden*, Adam and his family accept delivery of a Model T, is a wholly lovely thing. Steinbeck has always been the poet laureate of the jalopy. The subject is one he knows and loves. But just why do we have to interrupt the tale of Adam's decline and death, and the discovery by his sons of their mother's identity, for this pleasurable bit of Americana? Surely it is no more at home in this novel than it would have been in any except *The Moon Is Down;* and I would not put my hand in the fire that it was not originally conceived for one of the others.

The same can be said for such other chapters as the one which records the birth of the twins, the bloody fight of the Trask brothers, or the brutalizing and near-murder of Cathy—these among others. The question is not one of quality but of inevitability; one does not sense any dynamics of character or situation, any necessity which requires them to be where they are.

East of Eden repays the reading, but does so for incidental pleasures. Steinbeck writes well, as always, of the California land, of the task of working it, of the people—especially those who are briefly seen—who put their shoulder to the task. His minor characters, the mayors and doctors and storekeepers and brothel proprietors, are always interesting; one feels that if one could see them better they would be interesting indeed. And his boys are done as Steinbeck has always done them. In brief, whatever can be sketched is sketched beautifully; what is lacking is a central object which, for the length of a book, can stand contemplation.

In the books other than *East of Eden* he has been the Steinbeck we have so long known and liked—or more properly one of those Steinbecks in each of the books. In *The Pearl* he is the lover and defender and lyrist of the very humble, just as in *The Wayward Bus* he loves and defends and lyricizes the simple, hard guy like Juan Chicoy who is somehow as honest as the passengers he drives in his bus are not. And in *The Brief Reign of Pippin IV* he is Steinbeck the humorist, delighting in the combination of the humanly true with the humanly preposterous.

It would be ungrateful not to accept these later works for what they are, but it would be a major error—as well as very unfair to Steinbeck—to take them for Steinbeck's best. His best was better than these. His best was what he wrote in the days when he could not stand without indignation and see injustice done.

8
William Faulkner

the private vision

WILLIAM FAULKNER makes as many demands on his reader as
do our more difficult modern poets. His experiments—in perspective, in handling time, and in revealing (which is not the
same thing as *developing*) character—make it extremely hard
to tell what is happening in his stories. One also has difficulty
in telling whether what seems to happen is a real event or
merely the hallucination of one of the characters. Additional
difficulties are created by Faulkner's devices of withholding
bits of information the reader needs to piece the stories
together and of showing his characters in such a light that
while their motives are perfectly clear to the other characters the reader is left completely in the dark. Ninety-nine
characters out of a hundred seem driven by obscure obsessive
neuroses and tortured by anxieties which the reader does
not share and which lead to actions taking place outside the
normal order of events and at abnormal speed. And at moments there is an absurd disproportion between the stature
of the characters and the overwhelming horror of the things
that happen to them.

Faulkner has never consented to become one kind of
writer in the sense that Dos Passos is one kind of writer and
Hemingway is one kind of writer. And to make the reader's
problem more difficult, there has not infrequently been a
feeling of improvisation about his work, as though he felt

that this was the best he could do for now and he would try
to do better again later, on a new job, starting with a clean
slate. It is unnecessary to point out the places, in *Sanctuary*
for instance, where he sounds like someone swept away by
the discovery of his ability to write and so maddened by his
own perfume as to be unable to take the time to reread
himself.

Consequently criticism has had its troubles in giving a
full account of Faulkner's achievement. From a half-dozen
or so characteristics of the work as a whole it would seem
fairly possible to draw some conclusion as to just what he
has contrived to do with the American novel; but while such
characteristics turn up very frequently, no one ever turns
up twice in the same relationship to the others, and there is
always at least one of his novels in which it does not turn
up at all. And so, instead of trying to come to a complete
judgment of Faulkner, critics are likely to be satisfied with
a tentative and highly circumspect enumeration of some
peculiarities of his work—the peculiar optics, his attitude
toward personality as a gathering-lens for impressions, and
his unusual manipulation of time, together with the effect
of these things upon his style, the technical feats they make
possible in the creation of atmosphere and tension, and their
close relation to the things he is able to do in the way of
exploiting ambiguity, absurdity, and violence.

Quite probably the most important of these characteristics is Faulkner's habit of seeing the action through the personality of one, or several, of the characters in the particular
story, to whom another novelist would be unlikely to entrust
the "point of view." This may or may not make life difficult
for the reader. In *Intruder in the Dust* we get the action
through the eyes of a single person, an adolescent boy, and
once we have learned who and what he is, there is no trouble;
but it is necessary to read well into *The Sound and the Fury*

before one realizes that the incoherence of the first part is caused by the fact that the narrator is literally an idiot, and no sooner do we have this straightened out than we have to follow through Quentin's last day in Cambridge and we blunder along because we are not aware that this is the Cambridge of a youth on his way to commit suicide. In *As I Lay Dying* Faulkner complicates the task even further, by passing the narrative round and round the circle of the dramatis personae; you see the characters through the eyes of each of the other characters in turn, so that the action moves forward in a sort of spiral. In *Sanctuary* the whole effect of this is almost like watching a movie wherein the action is photographed three or four times, from different angles, with different lightings, at different speeds. The reader suffers with Temple Drake through her first night on Lee Goodwin's farm, while a procession of ominous characters moves in and out of her room; but it is only much later in the book and from another character, in a rehash of the same night, that one finds out what actually happened—all because during that night Temple is too frightened and confused to be clearly aware of what does go on around her. And in the same way, one does not learn until some time after the event about what happens in the famous incident with the corncob, because Temple is simply aware that *something* is happening; only when she is installed at Miss Reba's does she find out what it was. Meanwhile, of course, a great deal has been revealed about Temple's character. Here we have one of the great advantages of Faulkner's optics. The corresponding disadvantage is that to understand what he is reading the reader has to wait an inordinately long time for the information he really needs.

Certain of Faulkner's characters, like the famous Popeye, and Lucas in *Intruder in the Dust,* are never permitted to view the action at all; we never see it through them. Others, like Chick in *Intruder,* are almost completely agents of the author; whenever they are present we see only what they see, and we are not permitted to see them through the personality of another character. The rest of Faulkner's people are at once contemplated and contemplators—we see them through other characters and we see the other characters through them. Their presence is what makes the great complexity of some of the novels.

And it is also the central factor in Faulkner's technique. For the characters who stand as Faulkner's agents are essentially vast recording machines of impression. Faulkner works, through them, very close to the brute stuff of consciousness. Sensations are reported with extreme immediacy. But sometimes we have to wait, through whole pages and chapters, to know their importance. Since the flow of sensations rarely decelerates, there is seldom time for interpretation. Thus the style becomes an extraordinary sort of indirect discourse —extraordinary because while Faulkner is immensely occupied with the sensations of the characters (to such an extent that frequently his writing would be much clearer if he would preface a paragraph with an explanatory "he sees" or "he feels"), the language in which the sensations are reported is rarely that of the characters and frequently is so different from any language his characters could ever use that the unforewarned reader finds it ridiculous.

At this point, what Faulkner does is just the opposite of Dos Passos' careful effort to put the indirect discourse into language appropriate to the character. Whenever the sailor, Joe Williams, enters the story of *The 42nd Parallel,* the entire vocabulary of the narrative drops into a set of words that Joe Williams himself would use. Contrast with Dos Passos' practice something like the following: "Fonzo thought of himself surrounded by tier upon tier of drawn shades, rose-colored, beyond which, in a murmur of silk, in panting whispers, the apotheosis of his youth assumed a thousand avatars."

Fonzo has just arrived in Memphis from the country so green that he has mistaken the latticed entrance of Miss Reba's place for a privy, and is still unaware that what he had thought was a lodging house is in fact a cathouse. Avatars? Apotheosis? The words are even less "appropriate" to Fonzo than they would be to Joe Williams.

This aspect of Faulkner's style has, from time to time, trapped critics who are ordinarily among the more perceptive into the judgment of his writing which amounts to saying that people do not talk "like that." One must allow, however, that unless we consider Faulkner as working within a convention to which a realistic criterion does not apply, the judgment seems fully justified. I am far too fond of Faulkner's work to be able to agree that *Sanctuary* is the irretrievable mess that some have called it, but the book does in fact contain passages which seem designed to mislead the inexperienced reader—to whom, unless he has the good luck to tumble immediately to the secret justification of such prose, they are bound to suggest that the novelist failed to reread his first draft.

The narrow stairwell turned back upon itself in a succession of niggard reaches. The light, falling through a thickly curtained door at the front and through a shuttered window at the rear of each stage, had a weary quality. A spent quality; defunctive, exhausted—a protracted weariness like a vitiated backwater beyond sunlight and the vivid noises of sunlight and day. There was a defunctive odor of irregular food, vaguely alcoholic, and Temple even in her ignorance seemed to be surrounded by a ghostly promiscuity of intimate garments, of discreet whispers of flesh stale and oft-assailed and impregnable behind each silent door which they passed.

The unforewarned reader is very likely to find this deliberately careless, purposely obscure, and formless. (William Van O'Connor, in *The Tangled Fire of William Faulkner*, assumes that I think the unforewarned reader to be right. I do not.) What he will see here is a mess of *mots impropres*, ambiguities, over-elaborations, preciousness, mixed metaphor, and dislocated syntax. What are the *niggard reaches* of the stairs, unless of course the expression means merely that the flight corkscrews up in a cramped space? What does *defunctive* add to *weary*? *Defunctive* happens to occupy an important place in Faulkner's vocabulary, but not in the sense of "funereal" which Webster gives it: in context it is hardly more than a tautology for *spent*, a piece of preciousness like that other one in the new preface of the Modern Library volume combining *The Sound and the Fury* and *As I Lay Dying*, in which Faulkner turns the idea of "having begotten a bum," into "being of a bum progenitive." And in what way is the weary quality of the light *protracted*?

Thus far the inexperienced reader has had to struggle only with the application of some loose adjectives. But now, in his innocence, the figures also begin to harass him. Only by the most devious kind of reasoning can he connect the *backwater* with the *vivid noises of sunlight and day*. The noise idea is really applicable to the light in the hall: in the sentence the noises belong by logic with the first term of the metaphor even though they are coupled by grammar with the second. Then in the next sentence *defunctive* reappears but this time not with an abstraction; applied to an odor, the word is easier to accept—even though "funereal," applied to food, involves some difficulty. Just what relation there is between the stale smell of food and the irregularity of its serving is conjectural and multiplicative, so to speak, of ambiguities. *Vaguely alcoholic* can be forced to give up its sense if, again disregarding syntax, we carry it back to *odor* and dismiss the invitation to couple it with *food*. *Ghostly*

6

promiscuity of intimate garments seems to be an intentional garbling of associations, conjuring up all the ambiguity of "promiscuous ladies' underwear"—*ghostly* because not actually present, *promiscuity* because the ladies who wear the garments are promiscuous. And finally, why does the *oft-assailed* flesh behind the *silent doors* have to be impregnable, when the silent doors exist only so the incessant capitulation of the flesh can take place in a lewd semblance of privacy?

Such paragraphs are common elsewhere in Faulkner. In fact, from the earliest writings right on down to *The Town,* there is hardly a book which does not contain similar specimens of style. The neophyte reader feels entitled to suspect that words sometimes get away from Faulkner as they never did from Tom Wolfe, that much abused man who knew perfectly well what his words meant and merely used too many of them.

But the worst has not been said about the paragraph, *as realism.* This is a description of a cathouse, which will be the scene for a most important part of the story. And we are not permitted a clear view of the locale, with the result that the documentary element is obscured. We are not even permitted to deny that things are "like that," because we are unable to discover what it is that we are denying.

Precisely! It is hardly a part of Faulkner's method, or of his intention, that we should. As veteran Faulkner readers know, there is a proper way to read this passage: to pay no more attention to the surroundings than Temple Drake pays. You are seeing through the eyes of an abducted girl who has been shut up in a brothel. She has been raped by a perverted maniac. A brainless, magnolia-blossoms-and-helplessness coed in all the possible implications, she has been through a phantasmagoric experience which has left traumata all over her mind and body. She is nothing but an amorphous slither of incoherent impressions—and a complete moral paralysis. When the whorehouse hall is seen as she sees it, the fact that the metaphors are incoherent becomes unimportant and the incoherency itself becomes functional to the writing. Because her mind is in no condition to select between meanings, the ambiguities become appropriate. The inexactitude of the figures and the scrambling of the adjectives reflect the powerlessness of an inferior mind to grasp and identify its surroundings. The style is tuned to a character who is a part of Faulkner's world. Miss this fact and you miss the meaning of much that he writes.

Grant Faulkner his own convention—he has written that he sees no reason why what is in the mind of a character must be revealed in words natural to that particular mind—and there is no need to worry about the appropriateness of his language (in the realistic sense); and at the same time the door is opened for the peculiar, and immensely successful, doubling of the "point of view" which characterizes Faulkner's fiction and is one source of his unique power.

Here is Gavin Stevens speaking:

... The New Englander is too of course back inland from the coastal spew of Europe which this country quarantined unrootable into the rootless ephemeral cities with factory and foundry and municipal paychecks as tight and close as any police could have done it, but there are no longer enough of him just as there are not of the Swiss who are not a people so much as a neat clean small quite solvent business ...

Now on the face of things no man, not even the Harvard-Heidelberg educated attorney of Yoknapatawpha County, is supposed to speak like this. The words are much less a speech that Chick Mollison hears than the account of the effect of a speech on a tired, nervous boy who has been out all the previous night digging up a corpse and is now being lulled by the motion of a motor car. The ideas are among those over which Gavin Stevens broods throughout *Intruder*. But the language itself is Faulkner's; the style is unmistakable; "this country quarantined unrootable into the rootless ephemeral cities" is almost a signature. Gavin Stevens is brooding . . . in Faulkner's voice, and we have the curious feeling of hearing the two of them together.

One must concede at once, of course, that Faulkner's practice is not entirely consistent throughout the canon. Some of the novels—most obviously *The Sound and the Fury* and *As I Lay Dying*—attempt a high degree of dramatization, with the author disappearing more fully from his pages. But taken by and large, and coming up from the novels of the late twenties to *A Fable* and *The Town*, a language which is more Faulkner's own than that of whatever character he happens to lend it to pervades the work and binds book to book in an inclusive unity. Faulkner's annals of Yoknapatawpha County get their cohesiveness not only from a common scene and a common material, but also from this common style. It is true that certain critics of stature—including, I believe, Edmund Wilson—have never been able to accept the style as a viable one. They do not, however, deny the unifying function of the style in the work as a whole.

I would suggest that the style, and the unusual treatment of the "point of view" which the style permits, are organically related to the characteristic treatment of time which marks so much of Faulkner's writing. For in the flow of impressions which come to us through the mind of the character the ordinary distinction between past and present is frequently missing. The character lives in and focuses his attention on the present, but mixed in the surging sensations of his mind are reminiscences of the past, brought to the surface by the stimulus of present sensations, which impinge upon the present and become part of it. Thus in *Intruder*, the knowledge

that old Lucas has been accused of murder brings back
across Chick's consciousness the four-year-old events of his
fall in the brook and his rescue by Lucas, the meal given
him at the Negro's house, his host's refusal to take pay—
the whole incident which accounts for Chick's attitude
toward Lucas and the murder and explains the sources of
the old anxiety state, now revived in Chick by the news of
the crime. This is not quite the same as the movie-like flashback which explains some present turn in the narrative; it is
much less "background" than part of the stuff of the present,
because, in movie terms, the present does not disappear from
the scene as it does during the flashback; instead the two
actions are, as it were, projected on the screen simultaneously.

The notion of time that runs through Chick's mind toward
the end of *Intruder* comes very close to being the attitude
toward time which Faulkner assumes, very frequently
indeed, in his stories:

... yesterday today and tomorrow are Is: Indivisible: One (his
uncle for this too, anticipating this too two or three or four years
ago as his uncle had everything else which as he himself became
more and more a man he had found to be true: 'It's all *now* you
see. Yesterday wont be over until tomorrow and tomorrow began
ten thousand years ago....')

Conceiving time in such a way permits the existence of
two planes of action—one present and dramatic, the other
past and explicative but always influencing the present—
which form the pattern of the Faulkner novels which are
most original and most characteristically his. The present
plane catches the action at the beginning of a crisis and
follows through a catastrophe; the past one recapitulates
everything which makes the catastrophe inevitable. The
action of the present plane is likely to have the concentra-

tion and rapidity of good drama. In *Intruder* it covers, for practical purposes, one week end. In *Light in August* all the tumultuous action of a very much more complicated story than *Intruder* takes place in only ten days. On Friday Lena, riding into town looking for the man she will have to find quickly if he is to marry her before her baby is born, sees smoke rising from the burning Burden house. By evening of the next Monday but one everything is over; since the midnight before Lena arrived Christmas has committed his murder, the man hunt has chased him to earth, Hightower has been brought out of his reclusion, old Hines has come to Jefferson to demand the retributive blood of his own grandson, Byron Bunch has thrown up his job to follow Lena, Lena's baby has been born, and Percy Grimes has murdered Christmas. And meanwhile, on the other plane, we have had the tortuously unfolded stories of how the principal characters got the neuroses which have brought them here, each according to the inexorable law of his own personality, to make the catastrophe inevitable. Out of this past come the obsessions and anxiety states of the characters which stand in the place of motives, determining their conduct.

And this past is the history of the South, treated as what Mr. Cowley called Legend and what I would rather call Myth, myth being an account of origins which explains why things must be as they are. Hightower, the unchurched minister, is what he is because a soldier-ancestor died an ignominious death in a henhouse in this town. Christmas' role is determined for him by the putatively Negro man who made Milly Hines Christmas' mother. The Burden woman is murdered because a harsh white man named McEachern once prayed for Christmas. And so forth.

But very often the characters do not know whether what they are thinking has to do with the present or with the

past. Here, for example, is Hightower as he listens to the
steps of his friend Bunch retreating in the night.

...He is thinking quietly: "I should not have got out of the
habit of prayer." Then he hears the feet no longer. He hears now
only the myriad and interminable insects, leaning in the window,
breathing the hot, still, maculate smell of the earth, thinking of
how, when he was young, a youth, he loved darkness, of walking
or sitting alone among the trees at night. Then the ground, the
bark of trees, became actual, savage, filled with, evocative of,
strange and baleful half-delights and half terrors. He was afraid
of it. He feared; he loved in being afraid. It was as though a door
had shut somewhere. He was no longer afraid of darkness. He just
hated it; he would flee from it, to walls, to artificial light. "Yes,"
he thinks, "I should never have let myself get out of the habit
of prayer."

Bunch has left after Hightower has failed to dissuade him
from a course of conduct which they both feel to be wrong.
Hightower's sadness stems from this. But the stimulus of
the evening sounds and smells turns his mind back to the
source of the failure, which he attributes to the loss of his
feeling for the supernatural, the feeling of the imminent
presence of wrong. The key, I believe, is the word "maculate." What is a maculate, that is, a spotted, smell? Possibly
it means merely that the earth—by the workings of a sort
of synaesthesia—*smells* spotty. More likely, however, to a
man of seminary education like Hightower, maculate is the
opposite of *immaculate, without stain of sin* and thus the
woods smell here is suggestive of sinfulness. The habit of
prayer, ostensibly the theme of his meditation, has nothing
visible to do with either Hightower's youthful feeling about
woods at night or his failure to influence Bunch; what has
happened is that almost unconsciously he has let the presence of a smell take him back to the moment and the thing
in the past by which his failure at this present moment was
predetermined. It is in this sense that, as Gavin Stevens told

his nephew, "Yesterday won't be over until tomorrow." Probably it is needless to insist once more that these demands Faulkner makes on his reader—through style, point-of-view, time-handling, etc.—are so closely related as to be aspects of each other.

To all these obstacles has to be added the consideration that in those books where Faulkner is at his best, and which least invite comparison to Hemingway and/or Caldwell and/or Mark Twain, the characters through whom the story is narrated are for one reason or another under an unholy amount of stress. They are either the prey of obsession, like Hines, Hightower, and Christmas in *Light in August;* or tortured by a universe they cannot cope with, like the idiot in *The Sound and the Fury;* or frustrates, like Quentin and Benbow; or in the grip of an anxiety state, like Chick in *Intruder,* who is torn between the wish to mount a horse and get as far away as possible from all this trouble, and the compulsion to do something to square his account with the Negro Lucas. They reel under the shock of macabre circumstances: witness Anse Bundren and his family riding mile after mile with the mother's corpse, old Gowrie standing in the quicksand upon the body of his son, Chick and his companions opening the grave, and McCarron's decomposed body being recovered from the hollow tree. They feel the impact of the violence which they perform, like Christmas —or witness, like Hightower—or receive, like Temple Drake. And they are aware of being either the agents, or in danger, of an evil which is always abroad in the world, incarnate sometimes in an individual, sometimes in a mob, sometimes in nature itself. Even in books like *The Hamlet* there is someone palpably capable of bringing catastrophe upon himself and the other characters; and, whether within the story he actually does so or not, the possibility is always implicit. Consequently, the minds of the characters can almost be said to move not in two merging time-planes but in three, their constant apprehension over what is imminent constituting what amounts to a third temporal dimension.

It is undoubtedly the omnipresence of this always-imminent, nameless evil that gives the best of such books their fascination and power, their ability to terrify and attract at once. Perhaps its workings (never its nature) are plainest in the case of Percy Grimes, the man who missed being in the war and wants nothing but to be a soldier. He commands the guard which is formed to preserve order when Christmas is in the jail; and when Christmas breaks away from his jailers, Grimes is the natural leader of the pursuit. Between him and the man he is chasing he feels the strange fellow-feeling which the natural-born hunter feels for his quarry. "Good man!" he applauds within himself when Christmas, almost cornered, manages once more to slip away. But then, horrifyingly, when he has Christmas at bay behind the upended table in Hightower's kitchen, this man turns not only executioner but butcher, and having shot his helpless victim seizes the kitchen knife and castrates him. The unusual horror of the action rises from the fact that when we first meet him, late in the story, Percy Grimes is not only an insignificant figure but a somewhat comic one. Between his stature and the size of the awful thing he does there is a fundamental disproportion; it is absurd in the same way that it is absurd for the feckless, vapid Temple Drake to bring down upon herself and those associated with her the catastrophes which fill *Sanctuary*. The point is that to Faulkner the absurd is the rule and may be counted on as part of the human condition. It is, in a way, the agent of the omnipresent evil.

What Faulkner does with Percy Grimes is very similar to what other writers, Stribling and Caldwell for example, have done with mobs. By convention the mob consists of individuals who of themselves would be incapable of doing the frightful things a mob does. The mob is capable of them, because somehow in the stimulation of mass excitement it acquires a personality of its own, and embodies an evil potential which its constituent individuals do not possess. We have socio-psychological labels which explain, and thus in a way make bearable, what happens. But Faulkner makes the same transmutation from harmless fool to homicidal hysteric take place within the individual himself, while we are watching him—and we lack the convenient label to relieve our *Angst* by identifying the nature of his conduct. He acts that way because he is a man. Apparently there is much besides the Kingdom of God within us.

Such balefully evil characters as Popeye in *Sanctuary* are something else again. Popeye is sick. The evil in him is a physiological product, the result of one of nature's slips. This seems to be the source of the greatest single weakness of *Sanctuary*: we discover, at the very end of the book, that the evil which has harassed us from the beginning has been bogus; we have been flimflammed into taking seriously what turns out to be, at best, melodrama. Faulkner's basic technique consists of keeping the reader incompletely informed not about the action itself, but about motive. Had the reader known earlier about Popeye's bad heredity, most of the thick "Gothic" atmosphere of the piece would have disappeared. The novel has more uncertainty and uneasy suspense than it has justification for the suspense. One suspects that Faulkner's habit of creating such tensions is rather automatic than reasoned.

We may be putting a finger, here, on a serious weakness in Faulkner's work. There is a line to be drawn, somewhere, between the obsessive neurotic and the individual who is, so to speak, just slightly cracked. And sometimes Faulkner may be passing off the second for the first. A Bayard Sartoris

seems to me to become increasingly less interesting, and less
worthy of the tone in which Faulkner treats his story, as the
evidence gradually leaks out that his trouble is no tragic
obsession but an inability to "settle down" after the more
or less routine psychic maladjustments and dislocations of
war service. And the frighteningly single-minded Snopeses
of *The Hamlet*, with their barn-burning and their determination to turn everything to their own use, turn into the somewhat comic eccentrics of *The Town*. Such disappointments
in Faulkner's characters turn up infrequently, but just often
enough to encourage the feeling that sometimes the tension,
and the feeling of evil, are mechanically contrived (by not
telling the reader what he needs to know) and a little
spurious.

This objection, however, does not alter the fact that
many other characters in Faulkner's work carry evil with
them, or in them, without being in any way contrived. Even
in *Sanctuary*, Popeye is not the unique agent of evil; misfortune, catastrophe, and death follow Temple Drake wherever she goes. The extent of her responsibility is, of course,
dubious, but even so the expiation she finally manages, in
Requiem for a Nun, seems morally appropriate. Occurring
more frequently in Faulkner's work than characters like
Popeye, characters like Temple Drake seem to carry the
potentiality of evil within them merely because they are
human, and as human beings creatures of the absurd. In
As I Lay Dying, old Anse Bundren, after the anguish of
the trek across country with his wife's body to bury her
where she wanted burial, turns out to have spent the money
his daughter was saving for an abortion to buy some store
teeth so that he can court a new wife. One senses in this
something wildly comic, at which, if one could only view
the action from a great enough distance, one could laugh.
But one cannot, staying on the planet, get that far away,

and this is, consequently, the comic at which laughter is impossible—i.e., precisely, the absurd. The patently absurd individual, like Anse Bundren, is capable of any evil. Idiot Ben, in *The Sound and the Fury*, might have harmed the children whom he frightened, but there is equal possibility that his brother Quentin (who commits suicide in Massachusetts), or his nymphomaniac sister Caddie, or her wild daughter Quentin, or even the less ominous moneygrubbing brother Jason, would all do as much. In the world as the realist sees it, the world of ordinary experience, ordinary people do bad things proportionate to their size.

To an earlier generation the word evil, if it meant anything at all, meant a product, something spawned by economic forces or by society, something man-created and incidental, certainly not one of the residual data of human nature. For Zola evil came from the political and social corruption of the Second Empire; it could be controlled by suppressing the Empire. For Dreiser, evil was the System, the Great Machine; his social views aimed at its elimination by restriction of the effects of the Machine. The disparity between this and Faulkner's attitude toward evil should in itself show how far Faulkner is removed from the traditions of realism.

We have recently returned to a still earlier generation of writers, like Hawthorne and Melville, because of their awareness of the presence in the world not of things each of which can be called *an* evil, but of evil *tout court*. Our renewed interest in these authors is to be explained in part by the fact that in our lifetime something very like a personification of evil has walked the earth. For a while Adolf Hitler made a very serviceable proxy for the Devil. We uncovered Buchenwald. And if we averted our eyes from things like Buchenwald, it was not merely because the sight was unpleasant. Buchenwald institutionalized and organized something which was not exclusively German and which was far from unfamiliar to America. Between what happened to millions of Jews in the Nazi death camps and what happens to a lynched and burned American Negro the difference is merely numerical. We live in anxious awareness of our own guilt. We find in ourselves traces of the same potentiality of evil which marks the characters in Faulkner's novels.

The variety of demands which Faulkner makes on his reader doubtless explains why we have been so slow in perceiving the variousness of his talent. That we are in fact aware of the variousness is incontestable. A generation of critics which sees symbols everywhere has discovered in Faulkner a purveyor of its favorite commodity. We have learned to see beneath the surface, to recognize in *Light in August* the structural outlines of the Grecian Urn and in Lena the unravished Bride of Quietness. Another band of researchers has unearthed a Faulkner preoccupied with a somewhat existential kind of Protestant theology. Still others see him as a mind possessed by the decline and possible regeneration of the South. And Faulkner the humorist also emerges, to assume for some at least the legitimate succession of Mark Twain.

The situation at this writing is one to make an observer revise his views on the problem of the chicken and the egg. For if Faulkner's earlier claim to some of these distinctions was hazy, he has moved in recent years to become what his interpreters say he is: *A Fable* should satisfy any addict of allegory; Gavin Stevens, in *Intruder in the Dust*, becomes the voice of the Concerned Southerner whose conscience struggles with the Problem; *The Town* revives, after many years, the story of the Snopesian New Order usurping the place of the Old—and is replete with symbols and turns of humor.

This is certainly a far remove from the day when we thought of Faulkner as the creator of a turbulent private world, and one who was in constant danger of being misunderstood by readers who assumed that he was offering them not this private world but a misleading picture of a public one, not one man's feeling of the South but a South which any man at all would feel. It is good that the change has come about. Good also is the transformation wrought by the last decade, the Nobel prize, the wide diffusion of Faulkner's writing in reprint, and the efforts of an active and admiring criticism, all of which have conspired to turn Faulkner from the least publicly familiar of consequential American writers into a recognized and admired public figure.

Yet it is doubtful, even so, that what Faulkner has written since 1950 has done much toward the definitive shaping of his reputation. As he has bent, more and more, toward an explicit concern about the social welfare of the South, Faulkner seems to have been able to muster much less creative energy. *Intruder* suffers from the division of interest between the private anguish of the adolescent Chick and the public pronouncements of the author through his mouthpiece, Gavin Stevens. *The Town* suffers from permitting us too much familiarity with the Snopeses: it breeds contempt. In *The Hamlet,* where they are seen from a distance, they frighten us: nothing, including murder, stands between them and dominance; they move in like a virulent disease, and if you put one of them down two, at the very least, rise up to occupy his place. But in *The Town,* while Flem Snopes finally manages to drive De Spain from the presidency of the bank and thus to place himself at the head of the institution identified with old Colonel Sartoris, Flem himself becomes too much a comic "character," and exists too exclusively for the fascinated amusement of V. L. Ratliff. If these people appeared formerly to sum up what has happened to the South and to be the protagonists of a culture clash of momentous proportions, they now seem too trivial to justify the attention they have gotten. *A Fable*, meanwhile, puzzles more than it edifies. The allegory seems inarticulate: the book as a whole has the effect of a man saying something so important that he can't get the words out of his mouth. Criticism may in time make something of this account of a manifestation of the divine, but until now it has not done so. In other words, Faulkner's great works are still those like *Light in August, Absalom, Absalom!, Sartoris, The Sound and the Fury, The Hamlet*—the books in which he creates his tortured individual world.

Criticism has made a great point lately of the matter of individual worlds. We have had any number of books and articles under the title: "The World of So and So." Actually they are helpful, inasmuch as they insist that the exterior reality which was the meat of the nineteenth-century European realists was never objectively verifiable. Somehow we have lost a great deal of our confidence in "reality." But because of the usefulness of the idea of separate worlds as a critical concept, we have overworked it. We talk as though each of us moved in a world such that another individual would be lost in it. But we hardly mean this. Few of us really accept the extreme view of the nineteenth-century idealists that the world *is* because I see it and is *what* it is because I see it that way. We are more practical than that. We have to communicate with each other, and a substantial amount of agreement about the nature of the world is necessary for communication. We do agree in fact that we all see many things in the same way—by what we may call public vision. But at the same time, we admit that there is also a private vision, since all men see things more or less differently. This difference, the private vision, seems to constitute the subject of novelists like Faulkner.

Not completely, of course: public and private visions

interfere always to some extent, whence the never-ending confusion over realism and "faithfulness." They interfere very inconveniently in a book like *Intruder*, where Faulkner imposes upon one of his private-vision dramas the very public problems of the adjustment of the southerner to the rest of the world. The two types of vision blend poorly.

But when Faulkner is at his best and most characteristic, it seems, his private vision dominates the work. André Malraux, a percipient critic as well as a great novelist, says in the preface to the French translation of *Sanctuary* that Faulkner's achievement is to have blended the Greek tragedy with the detective story. The mystery-story part of this judgment is probably based on Malraux's reading of *Sanctuary*, and if so is merely incidental: Faulkner does not always fall into the pattern of the detective story. What Malraux says about tragedy, on the other hand, seems to be true of that large part of Faulkner's work in which his private vision is exploited.

For Faulkner's private vision is essentially tragic. Robert Penn Warren and others have insisted, rightly, that Faulkner's people are southerners only by geographical chance. Their lot, as Faulkner sees it, is the lot of the generality of men, Man's Fate: to be surrounded by evil, and inevitably, out of their own natures, to be both victims and workers of evil. As with the Greeks, the sign of evil is the violence it brings forth. Evil comes out of the past which a man cannot control—hence the drama recapitulating the Myth it grows from, the twentieth-century murder which has been foredoomed since 1861. A man may struggle against it, but he may not deny it or put it from him. The choices presented to him are really dilemmas disguised, and such victories as he wins are hollow.

Not all tragedy is luminous like the *Oedipus*. Some is dark with irrational fear, like the *Bacchae* of Euripides, in which a mother in religious frenzy helps tear apart the body of her own son, thinking him to be an animal, and appears before the spectators bearing what she still thinks is an animal's head. The quality of Faulkner's vision, his fundamental way of seeing people, seems to me to approach the Euripidean.

If we read him as though he were a tragic poet, many difficulties disappear. It becomes natural now that he should withhold much that the reader wants immediately to know, in order to prepare the recognition scene; that he should abandon the traditional time manipulation of the novel for one which turns the fullest, whitest light possible upon the moment of crisis; that characters should be driven to do things by forces which the reader understands only vaguely; that personal relations among the characters should be determined by their sense of the inevitability of the evil yet to come upon them; and that Faulkner's effort should go into showing how the world looks to his characters rather than how it should look to us.

In this light the novelist whom we honor as the finest writing in English today appears as a master of the "novel of destiny."

9
Ernest Hemingway

the river and the hawk

HEMINGWAY had the good fortune to discover early the discipline he required. He loved and admired Flaubert, and he wanted to achieve an accuracy of statement like Flaubert's—the difference between them being that whereas Flaubert had aimed especially at accuracy of statement regarding the exterior world, trying to nail an object with the one word that fitted it, for Hemingway the great necessity was to be accurate in the statement of emotions. Critics have rarely said much about this, although Edmund Wilson, whose chapter on Hemingway in *The Wound and the Bow* I admire, mentions it in passing. Yet Hemingway's varying career can be summed up in reference to this discipline. He adheres to it in the early short stories and the first two novels, and they are admirable. In the 1930's either *he* runs away *from* the discipline or *it* runs away *with* him; he preaches it, rather raucously, but has such great trouble with the practice that it is hard to admire much that he writes. And then, in a third stage, he returns to practicing it again, perhaps not with complete success.

From the beginning the thing that stirred him most was violence, and the emotions of which he wrote were those stimulated by pain and killing—war, and bullfighting, and big game-hunting, and fishing to kill rather than for sport, and love conceived as something in itself very akin to violence. Purposely he chose a material which was stronger stuff than that of Frank Norris, and wrote about it as Sherwood Anderson might have written, if Anderson, who was a great storyteller but a lazy artist, had not sloughed the job whenever a specific emotion was involved. The places where Anderson dodged, saying "that's another thing" or "but let that pass," are the ones in which by instinct Hemingway saw his major goal.

The discipline is present and full-grown in *The Sun Also Rises*, and becomes explicitly visible when the Paris episode is over and the characters have got into Spain. Jake and Bill are now on top of the bus from Pamplona to Burguete:

The bus climbed steadily up the road. The country was barren and rocks stuck up through the clay. There was no grass beside the road. Looking back we could see the country spread out below. Far back the fields were squares of green and brown on the hillsides. Making the horizon were the brown mountains. They were strangely shaped. As we climbed higher the horizon kept changing. As the bus ground slowly up the road we could see other mountains coming up in the south. Then the road came over the crest, flattened out and went into a forest. It was a forest of cork oaks, and the sun came through the trees in patches, and there were cattle grazing back in the trees. We went through the forest and the road came out and turned along a rise of land, and out ahead of us was a rolling green plain, with dark mountains beyond it. These were not like the brown, heat-baked mountains we had left behind. These were wooded and there were clouds coming down from them. The green plain stretched off. It was cut by fences and the white of the road showed through the trunks of a double line of trees that crossed the plain toward the north. As we came to the edge of the rise we saw the red roofs and white houses of Burguete ahead strung out on the plain, and away off on the shoulder of the first dark mountain was the gray metal-sheathed roof of the monastery of Roncevalles.

This comes extremely close to being a classic example of getting a maximum of effect from the least expenditure of

materials. Twelve of the eighteen adjectives are color refer-
ences, and remarkably unspecific; of the rest four are relatively empty—*barren, heat-baked, rolling, spread out*—and of
the other two, one tells you only that the shape of the
mountains on the horizon was strange. This leaves only the
metal-sheathed roof, and even here again, except in relation
to the others, there is nothing arresting. The adverbs—
slowly, steadily, higher—contribute no more. This is also true
of the verbs: *was-were* turn up thirteen times; most of the
others are simple statements about the movement of the bus
and changes in the countryside resulting from it. Only one,
ground, makes much of a sense impression, taken by itself,
and the sense impression is one which we are too used to.
Out of the others I find that I can get images as follows—
rocks sticking up out of the ground, a flattened road, cows
grazing, sunlight through trees, a road stretching away, fields
cut by lines of trees. And there is nothing in all of this,
except the mention of cork oaks and the monastery at the
very end, to identify the scene as specifically Spanish. You
can find most of the rest of it, even the red roofs, in the
American West.

At first glance the sentence structure presents the same
simplicity. But attempt complicating it and you see what
Hemingway is doing: change the three sentences from
"Making the horizon ..." as far as "... the horizon kept
changing," into "the brown, strangely shaped mountains that
made the horizon kept changing as we climbed higher," and
you discover that in doing it you have interfered with a
procession which has a characteristic orderliness and pace of
its own. Up to the moment when the bus comes over the
crest, Hemingway has been setting out straight statements
each containing one sense impression, with a full pause
after each, as the eye wanders farther from the grassless
shoulder of the road to the mountainous horizon, slowly,

with recognizable purposelessness. But presently the impressions become somewhat more specific. This forest above the crest is identifiable as cork oak; there are patterns of light and shadow; those are cows you see through the trees. And as he does this, the sentences become relatively more complicated, there is less pause between the impressions, and they are coming thick and fast when you at last see the monastery roof and know that it is Roncevalles and wake up to being in Spain.

In other words, the procession and pace here are essentially emotional. We now remember how the ride started. The two men are on the bus with a number of Basque country people, among whom Jake feels especially at home. We get the feeling that to Hemingway, unspoiled people of this sort are always good. (See his treatment of the African tribe in *Green Hills of Africa* for the type of primitive he likes particularly.) Wineskins have passed around. Jake and Bill are happy and full of good fellowship, completely relaxed and certainly mellowed by the wine. They are watching the view without paying any special attention to it until the bus nears its destination, where they have the right to expect a great deal of pleasure which they have come a long distance to get. Taken this way, the description makes particularly good sense; and a substitute job, full of color and precise detail and sharp, striking imagery, would be phony. Jake and Bill are in no mood for distinguishing between colors, or for looking closely at particular parts of the landscape, and their minds are too comfortable for them to be making any particularly acute associations which might produce metaphor. From this point of view, anything but what Hemingway has produced would be emotionally faked, unnatural, a sort of impurity. Certainly there would be nothing hard or clean about it. This constant checking of the writing against the emotion involved is what I mean by discipline. It should be the central element in any discussion of Hemingway.

In the light of the discipline, the emotional pattern of the book as a whole becomes important; and we had better reconstruct it, since the passing of time is obscuring it more and more, at least to the new reader. The whole job of reading this book has changed from what it was when it came out. The Lost Generation has achieved the dignity— and unreality—of a historical concept. It is increasingly hard to remember that the American expatriates of the middle twenties were serious artists and not spoiled brats; it may be too much to expect that a group which fled America because it did not feel emotionally secure and at home there should seem anything other than trivial to another generation which, after a different kind of war, is compellingly impressed by the insecurity of mere *physical* life anywhere on the planet.

Certainly Hemingway's despair, like that of Eliot in *The Waste Land,* is the kind which can be contemplated with leisure and some ease; it is despair without terror. As a matter of fact, the years of the great depression blunted its point; too many people discovered that it is even more important to eat regularly than to feel quite in place among one's contemporaries. And consequently it is easy to miss the essential datum, that the emotional mood of the first part of *The Sun Also Rises* is a ceaseless, dull ache. The reader is supposed to know that Jake's physical disability is in large part a symbol for the general feeling of frustration and pointlessness of life, that if Jake were physically qualified to possess Brett it would make very little difference, that Brett's nymphomania is really unimportant because if she ever managed to overcome it she would be accomplishing the eradication of a symptom without doing anything for the sickness of the soul. I should think that it might be impossible for anyone opening the book now to find anything much, other than irrelevant digression, in the pages about the self-made Greek Count whose fantastic wine-parties, of course, used to have so much to do with the reader's getting the mood of the whole first part—since Jake so palpably feels that while such things are not a very profitable occupation they are certainly as profitable as anything else.

Yet only if we understand the essential emotional mood of the first part of the book can we appreciate the careful balance between the emotions and the writing—otherwise there is no reasonable explanation for Hemingway's writing so completely under wraps. We risk seeing much more of the snaffle and the bit than we do of the bloody horse. Either we feel the appropriateness of the constant toning down of the whole Paris episode or it will seem like a somewhat staged preparation for the Spanish part, designed to make the latter look brilliant by contrast. We have to know that we get a scant and referential treatment of the Paris scene because Jake is so used to it, and it is so much a part of his dull ache that he does not really see it. We get some of the free-associative spoofing that Hemingway loves to do, about taxidermy and the possibility of stuffed dogs as gifts, but this, as compared with the lovely examples of the same stuff in the Burguete episode, is carefully restrained. The characters do not yet appear as particularly interesting people; we know that Cohn is an importunate romantic oaf, that Mike Campbell is a drunken chronic bankrupt, that Brett is a drunk with a tendency toward promiscuity —and even of her we get something short of a full picture until the Paris episode is over and we discover that she has been sleeping with Cohn, for whom she cares absolutely nothing. Of them all we know just enough so that nothing they do later in the story will catch us by surprise.

Hemingway's whole method in this first part is pretty

well summed up in his description of Brett as she is riding with Jake in a taxi. It is night. Illumination is provided by an occasional shop window and by the flares of workmen who are repairing trolley tracks. All that you actually get of Brett (and here again Hemingway is sticking to his purpose of giving you what the character actually sees, not what he should see) is the whiteness of her face and the long line of her neck—even though these people are alone and they are as much in love as their personal disabilities will permit. Substitute in this instance the idea of emotion for light and you have Hemingway's guiding motive throughout the first part: he sees and says only what the abomination-of-desolation mood permits. Obviously, if the emotional climate should be lost on the reader, the whole point would also be lost.

For the emotional structure of *The Sun Also Rises* starts with the low-pitch of the Paris episode, and begins to rise when the people approach the Pyrenees. There is a general increase of awareness and a livening of the senses—the impressions we get from the page and a quarter describing the ride from San Sebastian to Pamplona are more intense than anything similar in the preceding ninety-five pages. The old ache remains, but emotions become more vivid and sense perceptions flow faster all the way through to the last day of the Pamplona fiesta; characters round out—as far as Hemingway's characters ever round out—and the clashes toward which they all have been heading take place. Then there is the magnificent account of the performance of Romero and Belmonte in the Pamplona ring; the party breaks up; Brett goes off with the bullfighter; and from here on to the end the emotions scale down into the old dull ache again.

What Hemingway does, having established the fundamental lack of integrity of Jake's friends Brett, Mike, and

Cohn, is to take them on the last brilliant days of the fiesta to witness a display—even though none of them seems qualified to recognize it or to profit by it—of the closest approach that he knows to perfect integrity.

Romero never made any contortions, always it was straight and pure and natural in line. The others twisted themselves like corkscrews . . . Afterward, all that was faked turned bad . . . Romero's bull-fighting gave real emotion, because he kept the absolute purity of line . . . Since the death of Joselito all the bullfighters had been developing a technic which simulated this appearance of danger in order to give a fake emotional feeling, while the bull-fighter was really safe. Romero had the old thing, the holding of his purity of line . . .

The fact of the great beauty of integrity is what, if I am right, makes the last day of the fights the climax of *The Sun Also Rises*. After this the story works down into the emotional doldrums of the dull ache in which it began, and the demonstration is completed that there is no new thing under the sun. In this interpretation of the novel, of course, Romero becomes even more than a man who pursues a dangerous trade with great integrity; he becomes a symbol for integrity itself. When Brett runs away with him after the fights, she is messing up something more important than the life of a promising young artist.

What Romero accomplishes with the sword and *muleta* is precisely what Hemingway wants to accomplish with words. In connection with the ride up from Pamplona to Burguete, we identified his discipline as a determined effort to be emotionally honest, to render the emotions pure, straight, real and unfaked; and we applied to his writing in that instance adjectives just now applied by Hemingway to Romero's performance with the bulls. We now have to emphasize the way in which Hemingway's ideal of integrity is connected with the act of violence and how, as a corol-

lary, being able to write well about violence becomes the
test of the writer's discipline.

For this purpose it is important that the spectacle of
integrity in bullfighting is double: beside Romero and his
artistic perfection we have Juan Belmonte, who cannot
match Romero even when unhandicapped and who, on this
day, is fighting in spite of the paralyzing pain of a fistula.
He is significant to this argument because in his case as in
Romero's, Hemingway, who, we say, has accepted a discipline of writing which forbids anything but the completely
unfaked feeling, lets his emotions run.

> ... Belmonte's jaw came further out in contempt, and his face
> turned yellower, and he moved with greater difficulty as his pain
> increased, and finally the crowd were actively against him, and
> he was utterly contemptuous and indifferent. He had meant to
> have a great afternoon, and instead it was an afternoon of sneers,
> shouted insults, and finally a volley of cushions and pieces of
> bread and vegetables, thrown down at him in the plaza, where he
> had had his greatest triumphs. His jaw only went further out.
> Sometimes he turned to smile that toothed, long-jawed, lipless
> smile when he was called something particularly insulting, and
> always the pain that any movement produced grew stronger and
> stronger, until finally his yellow face was parchment color, and
> after his second bull was dead and the throwing of the bread and
> cushions was over, after he had saluted the President with the
> same wolf-jawed smile and contemptuous eyes, and handed his
> sword over the barrera to be wiped, and put back in its case, he
> passed through into the callejon and leaned on the barrera below
> us, his head on his arms, not seeing, not hearing anything, only
> going through his pain.

Particular attention is invited to the last sentence of this
passage—which is actually half the quotation in length—
to the rushing summary of all the indignity and all the suffering, to the intuition of the defiant spirit of the man as
long as defiance is called for, to the eye of the writer fol-

lowing the minor detail of the sword wiping, and to the final overwhelming mastery of the pain. I do not know of any other place where Hemingway reaches such tension.

The figure of the bullfighter who for money, and for his own integrity, faces death with nothing but his courage left to carry him, comes up at least four times in Hemingway's work—here, and again in *Death in the Afternoon* with Manuel García Maera, who ruins his wrist by hitting bone with his sword but still goes on, try after try, until he has killed his bull, even though he has to use his left hand to pick up his sword each time it flies out of the grasp of his right; and in the case of the bullfighter in "The Undefeated" who returns to the ring when he is too old to fight; and in "Banal Story," which consists entirely of a bitter antithesis between the phony contents of the magazine *Forum* and the honest death of the Maera above mentioned, who dies in Madrid of pneumonia. This comes near to being a listing, to be put with the retreat from Caporetto in *A Farewell to Arms* and the story of the boxer in "Fifty Grand," of Hemingway's most effective writing.

The quality which makes men do these things Hemingway will later refer to as the quality of having *cojones;* one takes it there is thus a connection between having *cojones* and having integrity, and is consequently willing to put up somewhat with the protracted demonstrations of sexual stamina which make Hemingway's later novels at times sophomoric if not simply offensive. How plainly *cojones* symbolize the kind of integrity Hemingway admires, and was setting as a rule of discipline for himself in his early writing, becomes apparent even in the lamentable *To Have and Have Not*, in which Harry Morgan's lusty bed sessions are set up against the masturbations of the rich woman on the yacht and the adultery-for-profit of the aspiring writer. The discussion could even be extended to include speculations on the meaning of Jake's particular disability and the recurrent talk of steers in the middle part of *The Sun Also Rises*.

Meanwhile, the literary value of this sort of integrity comes home with all its force as soon as you pick up *A Farewell to Arms*. Strictly speaking, this book is hardly a novel at all, at least if the word novel is used in the traditional sense of a story which develops through the interactions of a group of characters one upon the other. For Hemingway's story has really but one major character, Frederic Henry, and is in the last analysis nothing more than the account of how falling in love feels to a young man who is sick of war. Few books are made of less material. Hemingway depends almost entirely on the trained and disciplined eye, and the carefully accurate report on the emotions. The end product may be—and I believe it is—closer to a good movie script than to a conventional novel: but it is still one of the few books of our time that stand entirely by themselves.

I do not mean exactly that Hemingway was working on this book, as I believe he was working on *For Whom the Bell Tolls*, with Hollywood production and even possibly a specific Hollywood actor in mind. I do mean that in large portions of the book his eye is working as the camera works when it is responsible to a good director. Time is relentlessly foreshortened: chapter one takes you through a whole fall and part of a winter of the war, in a series of rapid impressions briefly sketched, one flowing into another, by a sort of selection very much like that of the narrating lens. Then you narrow into the village and move into the officers' mess, to a table, and to a conversation which is significant only in that you know that this sort of thing goes on eternally. By the end of chapter three you have Henry back from his winter leave and spring coming on; what has intervened amounts to nothing—you know this from the stream-of-memory stuff, the familiar flashback technique which was probably an even more common device in the day of the silent film than it is now. The ambulance trips in the mountains are handled as if the camera were mounted on the truck.

We were in the foot-hills on the near side of the river and as the road mounted there were the high mountains off to the north with snow still on the tops. I looked back and saw the three cars all climbing, spaced by the interval of their dust. We passed a long column of loaded mules, the drivers walking along beside the mules wearing red fezzes. They were bersaglieri.

Beyond the mule train the road was empty and we climbed through the hills and then went down over the shoulder of a long hill into a river-valley. There were trees along both sides of the road and through the right line of trees I saw the river, the water clear, fast and shallow. The river was low and there were stretches of sand and pebbles with a narrow channel of water and sometimes the water spread like a sheen over the pebbly bed.

This is straight movie, complete with everything but the shooting directions, the lens being permitted to pick up more or less, and to hold it longer or shorter times, according to the mood of Frederic Henry. The technique is basically the same for the moment when the shell hits his dugout, for the Caporetto episode, for the row up the lake, for Catherine's death in the Swiss hospital. For the reader it all amounts to a remarkable feeling, at times almost painful, of the immediacy of the sensations.

Henry's mood, of course, is compounded of his disgust with the war and his love for Catherine Barkley. Just how scrupulously Hemingway reports this mood can be picked out of a comparison between two passages, superficially similar, which at first look like identical handlings of the stream of consciousness. One is the summary, mentioned above, of Henry's late-winter leave; the other the account of what runs through his head later on the same day, as he lies stretched on his bed waiting for supper. The first is a stream of jumbled memories of the one-night cheap hotels and the drinking and the whores, which added together make the story of his meaningless furlough. In the second he is becoming aware that he is really in love with Catherine; his fantasy fastens on taking her with him back to Milan, where he has just been, and each detail stands out alone in spite of the way they flood in on him.

Because we would not wear any clothes because it was so hot and the window open and the swallows flying over the roofs of the houses and when it was dark afterward and you went to the window very small bats hunting over the houses and close down over the trees and we would drink the capri and the door locked and it hot and only a sheet and the whole night and we would both love each other all night in the hot night in Milan.

The difference between the two passages lies of course in their representing two sides of a Romantic antithesis which is not at all original with Hemingway, a variation on the theme that the bravest are the tenderest; but the antithesis is stated here through a change in the manner of reporting sensations which has to be attributed to the essential discipline of the man and merits the adjectives we applied to the Burguete episode of *The Sun Also Rises*. This is the stuff *A Farewell to Arms* is made of.

Plus, to be sure, the inevitably deft dialogue and the unobtrusive insertion of a minor symbol here and there— for example, the rain. At the beginning of the book, the rain is only the misery of the soldier, a part of the ineluctable boredom of war. But after Catherine becomes pregnant we learn that she is afraid of "being dead in the rain." When the idyll is broken off and Henry has to go up to the front before Caporetto, they separate in the rain after the bleak experience in the station-side hotel. Rain falls on the whole Caporetto debacle, and Henry has to escape both the Italian battle-police and the rain-filled river; and finally, after everything is over and Catherine is dead, he walks away from the hospital in the rain. This manipulation of symbol does not, of course, diminish the book's value as a movie script.

Hemingway's position at the turn of the twenties was admirable. He had behind him two good novels, one of them (*The Sun Also Rises*) hailed more or less accurately as "speaking for a whole generation" and the other (*A Farewell to Arms*) destined to certain success in Hollywood; and the whole list of his early short stories, which critics might deny were stories in the accepted sense at all, but which succeeded time after time in nailing the emotional mood Hemingway was after, and were consequently things of beauty. Writers all over Europe and America would have been glad to have Hemingway's past for their future—and he was still a young man, with power to burn, and to develop.

But at this point a change came. Up to now there had always been, along with the other things, a perceptible moral aspect in Hemingway's work: what attitude should a man take toward a world in which, for reasons of the world's making and not of his own, he is fundamentally out of place? What personal happiness can he expect to find in a world seething with violence, endurable only at the cost of tolerating an abundance of pain which, unless one adopts a religious explanation, is meaningless? What values could one respect when ethical values as a whole seemed universally disrespected?

In a way, Hemingway may have been right in his conclusions—or at least in what we took to be his conclusions. Probably a world in which honesty turns out to be the only certain virtue a man can cling to, instead of one of the permanent data of human character of which one need not speak because it is assumed to be universally present, is in literal fact a hell of a world. America had been in a slough of materialism—shortly the material benefits would disappear, and we would all learn that we had spent a decade kidding ourselves. Certainly this world wherein the identifiable goods were few—friendship, nature, the thrill of action, and love of woman—and all of them very transient and always under tribute to war, pain, and death, could not be said to be much better after three thousand years than the world of the *Iliad*. In such circumstances honesty, integrity, or whatever one calls the ability to face the truth and tell it, was almost bound to become disproportionately important.

Now the need for integrity, out of which Hemingway had made a discipline and subjected himself to it, became for him a sort of refuge. His work had always displayed—as critics never tire of pointing out—a tendency toward such withdrawal. Jake in *The Sun Also Rises* has had a sort of retirement forced upon him; Lieutenant Henry's farewell to arms is a personal withdrawal from the war. Now in the thirties Hemingway begins to maintain that when you have served your time defending democracy and other similar intangibles, you have a right to go away afterward and do what is important to you. (One can only conclude that the defense of democracy and the other values whose defense is a constant concern to men of good will is, in this view, unimportant.) "The great thing," he writes in *Death in the Afternoon*, "is to last and get your work done and see and hear and learn and understand; and write when there is something you know; and not before; and not too damned much after. Let those who want to save the world, if you can get to see it clear and as a whole. Then any part you make will represent the whole if it's made truly."

This new emphasis is dramatic enough to invite any amount of amateur psychiatry, and amateur psychiatry is dangerous as a critical tool. I cannot help pausing, however, over the note of world-weariness here; it is as if we had a belated expression of the mood of *The Waste Land* and of *Ash Wednesday*. This sounds somewhat like another Aged Eagle reluctant to stretch his wings because they are no longer wings to fly but merely vans to beat the air. Actually Hemingway was only a ripe thirty-two in 1930, and the life he retired to was in fact the least retiring sort of retirement the world has yet seen in a man of letters: hunting mountain sheep, fishing for marlin, attending bullfights, and shooting big and dangerous game, always and everywhere in his goings and comings attended by the popping flashbulbs of publicity.

By retirement Hemingway meant mainly a change of attitude. He had never been one of those objective novelists who delight in the creation of character. In all three of the books of the retirement period, the central character is Hemingway; the other figures are there as a supporting cast. He appears as himself in *Death in the Afternoon* and in *Green Hills of Africa,* and in *To Have and Have Not* as Harry Morgan, the man who does everything (Freud would say "including die") that Hemingway would like to do. In the first two he is contemplating violence in the most striking forms he can find, at a time when, as he says somewhat regretfully, war is not available; and he is striving to report, still with the greatest possible accuracy, the emotions this violence inspires in him. Between the first book and the second, a further complicating factor intrudes itself. Hemingway now changes from the spectator, central and important, that he is in the bullfighting book; he becomes the participant—in the last two books, it is he who runs the danger and does the killing. It is as if he had come to final dissatisfaction along the line: to watch killing and to experience the associated aesthetic emotion is no longer enough; he must have the actual feel of the kill and the feel of the danger that attends it. On this subject, a passage on hunting is extremely

7

revealing. The hunters have wounded a buffalo which has taken cover, and are waiting for it to charge them:

This was different, this was no rapid fire, no pouring it on him as he comes groggy out into the open, if he comes now I must be quiet inside and put it down his nose as he comes with the head out. He will have the head down to hook, like any bull, and that will uncover the place the boys wet their knuckles on and I will get one in there and then must go sideways into the grass and he would be Pop's from then on unless I could keep the rifle when I jumped.

This grows more suggestive the more one studies it. Here is Hemingway, reporting with scruple the emotions he experiences at one of those moments of tension which fascinate him so much. He is waiting to be charged by a dangerous animal, and suddenly his imagination changes him from the hunter, which he is, to a bullfighter, which he isn't. He thinks of shooting down into the buffalo's chest, through between the shoulder blades where the matadors drive their swords, as he has just thought of the other buffalo he has killed in terms of a boxing image, and he has mastered his opponent to the extent that he can walk in and "pour on" punishment for the inevitable knockout. But now suddenly he realizes that this wouldn't work (the verb shifts into the conditional) and that if he goes through with his fantasy, not he but the white hunter with him will kill the buffalo. If Hemingway is telling the truth about his emotions here, the strange confusion of sports involved constitutes a most startling account of a man's wanting to identify himself with three figures of the killer. His wilful placing of himself in the way of violence will turn out later to be the chief reason—among a number—for the failure of *To Have and Have Not*, because it is related to the feeling one has, in reading this novel, that none of its happenings is in any way inevitable.

Almost everything he writes is exaggerated. The fine spoofing which is so natural a part of *The Sun Also Rises* and *A Farewell to Arms* now becomes the garrulous joking with the Old Lady interlocutor in *Death in the Afternoon*. The characters, already given to understatement and averse to intellection in the earlier novels, now descend to communication almost on the level of grunting. The tendency to reduce people to the animal level, always present in Hemingway, now results in a situation such as that in *Death in the Afternoon,* wherein the brave, integrity-filled bulls are almost superior, in Hemingway's own scale of human values, to the men who kill them. And the gift for semi-involuntary memory which gave us the page in *The Sun Also Rises* where Jake, lightheaded from being knocked out by Cohn, comes back to the hotel feeling as he used to feel coming home after a football game in which he had been kicked in the head—with his feet hardly seeming to touch the dead leaves along the gutter—now enters into the last chapter of *Death in the Afternoon,* from which you learn that Hemingway likes bullfighting in large part because of all the good times he has had in connection with it. Obviously, what Hemingway is mainly doing here is exploiting Ernest Hemingway.

To what extent he is doing so is apparent when even the careful gearing of the report of emotions to the intensity of the emotions themselves, so excellently done in the Burguete incident in *The Sun Also Rises,* now becomes almost a set technique. In the following, watch the emotions rise as Hemingway takes in the whole grace and beauty of the animal he has shot:

I looked at him, big, long-legged, a smooth gray with the white stripes and the great, curling, sweeping horns, brown as walnut meats, and ivory pointed, at the big ears and the great, lovely maned neck the white chevron between his eyes and the white of his muzzle and I stooped over and touched him to try to believe it . . .

Here the trick is done by the sudden removal of the punctuation, but the total effect is familiar. In *Death in the Afternoon,* the same device is being used to give you the emotions of a man who shouts at a bull:

If the bull in the pen below raises his great head with the wide horns, solid-looking and smoothly pointed and the hump of muscle on his neck and shoulders, heavy and wide in repose, rises in a great swelling crest under the black, hairy sheen of his hide and his nostrils widen and he lifts and jerks his horns as he looks toward the spectator then the amateur speaker of bull talk has had a success.

With all this, there remains a determination to tell the truth, to discern faking wherever it may be, that becomes almost pathological. Perhaps more of Hemingway's explanation of bullfighting is devoted to how to tell the fake stuff than to how to recognize the real. The same desire to get at true feeling, and true things, and how for example to kill in the honest and true way, runs through *Green Hills of Africa* and is always linked with the problems of writing: Hemingway's criterion of judgment becomes almost exclusively whether the writing is faked or real, and whether it is written simply enough so that any faking is discernible.

Ironically, for the first time in his career Hemingway himself begins to sound precious. In his earlier writing he mainly prefers direct statements to metaphor, and the rare metaphors the reader notices ring entirely true: for example, the figure in *The Sun Also Rises* which refers the slow, impeded movement of the crowd from the bull ring to the movement of a glacier. Now we get many more figures, some good like the one which refers the smell of sweat to the taste of a brass coin in the mouth, some less striking, like those repeated ones which refer animals' horns to wood, and some as labored as the facetious one in *Death in the Afternoon* which makes "the morning glory ... a floral monument of lasting endurance." The need for such ornamentation is something new and a little ominous: what worries us is less the presence of the ornaments than the fact that Hemingway should feel he needed them.

The actual shift from the novel to another form of writing had much less in it to worry us. *The Sun Also Rises* and *A Farewell to Arms* are novels only in a very loose sense of the word. Neither of them depends for its effect on the interactions of a group of characters. Jake's emotions are the center of *The Sun Also Rises*, and what happens in the book makes sense only when interpreted through Jake's personality. *A Farewell to Arms* is even more strictly the story of one man; here, even more than in *The Sun Also Rises*, the reader feels the cleft between the primary and the secondary figures. Both books have the foreshortening of time which is more properly the privilege of the drama than of the traditional novel—a technique toward which, since Hemingway demonstrated its immense value, American fiction has been striving with remarkable persistence. Back in the nineteenth century, when people like Henry James and Paul Bourget were taking such distinctions seriously, books like these would have been classified as *novellas*. I have some difficulty in feeling any wide gap between books in which Hemingway is reporting upon young men who are in character—tastes, occupations, age—very much like himself, and books in which he drops the pretense of fiction in order to discuss the same materials in definite reference to himself.

And why, to come directly to the main question, do we have to consider *Death in the Afternoon* and *Green Hills of Africa* such failures, anyway? One may not be particularly interested in bullfighting and still find that the considered statement, by an accomplished artist, regarding the effect

on his own personality of the study of the world's most
stylized form of violence is a document of extraordinary
interest, particularly if the artist is making a special effort
to see himself clearly at the time. Nothing prevents our
agreeing with Edmund Wilson that as a book about animals
Green Hills of Africa is dull, as we can agree with Max
Eastman that as a manual of tauromachy *Death in the Afternoon* is silly; we may still be passionately interested in
Hemingway's report on himself as a killer. I imagine the
answer is that we were concerned by the apparent disappearance of a novelist who seemed to be losing his grip. Hemingway himself was aware of the danger and discoursed upon it
for the benefit of the German traveler in the beginning of
Green Hills of Africa. He also seemed to feel the danger of
losing his memory for sharply characterized sensations, so
essential to his kind of writing. In the books after 1930 he
seems disproportionately intent on catching things before
he forgets them. Where most of the sensations recorded in
the earlier books are sights, he is now noting smells: smells,
for example, of the horns of dead animals, of the native
villages, of the trail where the buffalo have passed, of trees
where baboons have been sitting, of a new-shot sable. He
tries repeatedly to register the sensation of mixed exhaustion-
satisfaction coming after a kill. He studies out each element
in the series of sensations that follow the killing of a big
antelope: from the spreading in him of the alcohol from
the celebrative drink, to the eating of the fresh-killed meat,
to all the smells rising around the fire, to the growing relax-
ation, to wondering whether one of the natives perhaps does
not have an available sister. And repeatedly there is the
expressed concern lest the sensation be lost before it can be
set on paper. All this suggested, as did the various forms
of exploitation of himself in which Hemingway was indulg-
ing, that still another novelist whose promise was even

greater than his achievement was embarked toward a sterile middle age.

I am much more concerned about these books than about *To Have and Have Not*. I trust that it is possible to qualify as an admirer of Hemingway without having to admire this novel. Fundamentally it consists of two long short stories, obviously written separately and with only the personality of the hero to hold them together. As short stories, they may or may not belong with Hemingway's best; what is certain is that they do not belong in special proximity to each other. But Hemingway, like so many others in the middle thirties, had seen the communist vision: *To Have and Have Not* marks his emergence from the let-other-people-save-the-world mood into one of class consciousness, and the two stories, poorly glued together, become a class-conscious novel. Thus we get, sandwiched between the story of sword-fishing and the story of the Cuban revolutionaries, all the business about the rotten rich, with their masturbations and homosexualities and promiscuities, who haunt the same waters as Hemingway's hero. The great trouble with it all is that nothing Harry Morgan has done had to be done that way. There is no clear connection between the social-economic background and whatever it is that forces Morgan to kill Chinamen and Cubans for a living. He is a buccaneer—note that he is the namesake of two very brilliant characters, Morgan the pirate and Morgan the raider. The book is best read, if it must be read at all, as an adventure story. Occasionally there are flashes of authentic Hemingway, as for instance in the part where Mr. Johnson hooks, fights, and by his own carelessness loses the big marlin; but they are only flashes.

Those of us who really admired Hemingway had reason to be glad that *To Have and Have Not* was as feeble as it was, and so obviously an improvisation. It really proved nothing that we did not already know about him, and it left still open the great question, whether he really could revive his discipline and write another novel as good as the two he already had written. *For Whom the Bell Tolls* would shortly give us the answer.

The subject is ambitious enough in scope to make one mention Tolstoy and Stendhal and the much neglected Zola of *The Debacle*, even though it is focused on one local incident and takes its unity from its interest in the fortunes of one individual. The technical problem involved is the one Stendhal discovered when he had to write about Waterloo: that while the individual sees little, understands less, and knows almost nothing of a battle, the only other alternative is to postulate a more or less omniscient observer, with all this implies in the way of calling in post facto and inevitably false-ringing history to complete the panorama. But still, the subject was of the kind Hemingway needed. We know that he felt the challenge, that he felt that writing about war is one of the great tests, if not the greatest test, of a writer. In the sense that Flaubert said "Madame Bovary is me," Robert Jordan is Hemingway; *For Whom the Bell Tolls* is his chance to write on a subject he has lived in his full maturity, and it may be regarded as a full-dress performance.

Like Hemingway's other novels, this story grows out of an initial situation rather than out of the conflict of characters. Jordan has to die, from the start, because the stupid inefficiency and political maundering of the people on his side have to kill him. Golz is a good and intelligent soldier, and Golz has good reasons for putting Jordan in this fix, but Golz is not good enough to cope with the Fascists and his own side also; the irreparable lack of cohesion, the insubordinate and loose-tongued individualism, and the treachery of comrades in arms must throttle the offensive as surely as Jordan must blow the bridge. And if the offensive fails, Jordan will die.

In contrast with the mood of the earlier novels, the essential mood of the book is tragic. The characters are caught in a box from which there is no exit except through the inevitable violent catastrophe. We, the readers, know from the start what Robert Jordan suspects but hopes is not true, what he must as long as possible refuse to believe: that this is the last bridge he can ever destroy, that the role in which he has cast himself leads straight to the final and complete solution. The atmosphere—maintained by Hemingway at times through such an illegitimate device as the business of what Pilar sees in Robert's palm—is one of rapidly gathering doom, heightened and driven home by the destruction of El Sordo's group, the defection of Pablo, the threatened defection of Pilar.

Admittedly the tragedy is, in William Empson's sense, pastoral. The characters, Jordan included, are all simpler personalities than is the reader, and fail for this reason to give the reader any feeling that these are people entirely like himself. I suppose that this makes them swains—but certainly not mere creatures of an imaginative convention. Like Steinbeck's Joads they all understand, at least in part, that a Force is driving them to the catastrophe. Jordan has the rich understanding of his plight that marks the tragic hero, even though he is unable to put in words his whole conception of why it is basically right for him to be where he is. And at the end, his understanding of the story becomes one with the reader's, so that the tragic irony—the discrepancy between the hero's understanding of his misfortune and the audience's understanding of it—is resolved. The reader has no trouble in identifying himself satisfactorily with Jordan through their common humanity; he admits that, in true fact, this man's death diminishes him; pity and

terror are legitimatized. Thus our emphasis falls less on
pastoral than on tragedy.

Meanwhile, the treatment of time is dramatic, and lends
itself to the building of tragedy. I have no doubt that Hemingway was "writing for Hollywood," and that one reason
for keeping everything in this book within the scope of four
fully-packed days was his wish to be sure the action of
the script would not drag. It still remains that this is a way
of securing a maximum of dramatic impact on the reader.
The reader is focused on the actual moment of the story,
almost on the line at which the future joins the present; his
apprehensions center always on what is going to happen in
the moment next to come. What is past is handled by movie
flashbacks; it is not significant for itself but only for the
meaning which it adds to the present action. This is significant, rather than astronomical, time. We have to accept
the fiction, as Robert Jordan wants to accept it when he is
with Maria, that a man can live out the meaning of his lifetime in a few revolutions of the hour hand. It is a fiction, a
time-concept, by the way, which we accept unquestioningly
in any number of American short stories, including some of
Hemingway's own such as "The Short Happy Life of Francis
Macomber." Hemingway has not used it in his earlier novels.
In fact, the argument that time is fundamentally insignificant
is basic to *The Sun Also Rises,* and the only importance of
time in *A Farewell to Arms* is related to the cycle of human
gestation. But these novels were written before American
novelists—Steinbeck, Faulkner, sometimes Caldwell—moved
into such close alliance with the drama and the movie.

I have more than a mere suspicion that Hemingway's
fundamental discipline in writing—which still holds for
this book (Robert Jordan has been engaged in writing a
"true" book about Spain; the ambition echoes all that Hemingway has said first and last about writing only what one

knows, reporting what is seen instead of what one by convention ought to see, feeling only what one actually feels)
—stands in basic conflict with the necessities involved in
writing a long novel in which there are other important
characters than the hero. It is not natural, or lifelike, or
"realistic" for Pilar to describe the violent opening of the
revolution and the murder of the local Fascists as she does.

> ... Then the two lines fell back and let him lay the dust over
> the center of the plaza; the hose sweeping in wide arcs and the
> water glistening in the sun and the men leaning on their flails or
> the clubs or the white wood pitchforks and watching the sweep
> of the stream of water. And then, when the plaza was nicely
> moistened and the dust settled, the lines formed up again and a
> peasant shouted, 'When do we get the first Fascist?'

Take this out of quotes and it is straight Hemingway,
not Hemingway seeing the thing through his character's
eye, but the character seeing it through Hemingway's. As
one follows the whole story of the uprising, the feeling grows
that it is always Hemingway talking, rather than Pilar, and
eventually one comes to wonder what all this is doing in the
present story anyway, since it has nothing to do with Robert
Jordan's story nor very much to do in revealing the character
of Pilar, and is much more than is needed to prove that the
sadly shrunken Pablo was at one time a whole man. The fact
of the matter is that the uprising is a wonderful invitation to
write about particularly shocking violence for its own sake,
and one which Hemingway cannot resist. I am not here
questioning its quality as a detached piece of writing; the
point is that it should have been physically detached from
For Whom the Bell Tolls and included in an appendix. But
this would not obviate the whole difficulty. Pilar has not
only Hemingway's way of seeing things; she also has his
afición, has like him frequented bullfights, and we get all

UNIVERSITY OF WINCHESTER
LIBRARY

the long pages about the declining weeks of the life of
Finito, a somewhat latter-day version of Juan Maera except
that instead of pneumonia Finito has tuberculosis.

There is also a chance that Pablo, like Pilar, is at times
merely an aspect of the character of Hemingway. Pablo
is the man who can see too clearly how things are going to
come out, who loses any fervor he has left and decamps,
only to return at the last moment, for reasons which he cannot explain very well, to participate in the attack on the
bridge. This so clearly sketches the outlines of Hemingway's
own career in political liberalism over the years—his partici-
pation in making the world safe for democracy, his subsequent withdrawal (let those who want to save the world),
his eventual angry return—as to make it seem that in Pablo
Hemingway is expressing a side of himself that he could
not well put into Robert Jordan.

Meanwhile the multitudinous garrulity which annoys
readers of the Hemingway books of the 1930's now turns
up in the interior monologues of Hemingway's hero. Robert
Jordan's preoccupation with his family, particularly with
the bravery of his Civil War veteran grandfather and the
suicide of his father, runs on interminably. He probes the
reasons and relives the events, fascinated with the problem
of his father's cowardice now that he, the son, runs such
fearless risk of death. Suicide, of course, is a violation of
what we have seen as Hemingway's notion of integrity,
being a failure either to live with courage against the odds
of life or to die with *cojones,* as Jordan himself will die. To
this extent Jordan's interior monologue is a continuation of
the longer discussion of courage that has always bemused
Hemingway, and the subject has grown on him just as
boyhood reminiscence has grown on him—compare Jordan's
verbose flashbacks to American boyhood with the brief one
in *The Sun Also Rises* where Jake remembers how he felt

after the high-school football game. The fact of the matter seems to be that over the years Hemingway, whose earlier work had been extremely reticent even when the basic material—especially in the early short stories—was palpably autobiographical, has given way to the romantic need for confession, has become an *homme qui se raconte.*

This is too bad, because all this is just another way of saying that Hemingway's personality, his basic exhibitionism, foils his intent as artist. Obviously the great departure of this book from his earlier ones is that here he is attempting a work with scope enough to hold important characters other than himself. He has not tried this before. Nick Adams in the short stories, Jake, Frederic Henry, and Harry Morgan are, as I have already pointed out, in one way or another, facets of Hemingway's public personality; but this does not seem particularly illegitimate in the respective situations in which they appear. In *For Whom the Bell Tolls*, on the other hand, there is a feeling almost of frustration as the author peeks in turn out of each of his major characters. The people who stand alone are the minor ones: Sordo, Anselmo, Agustín, Karkov. The less we see the character, the less he looks like Hemingway.

One regrets these things because otherwise the book is so good. The chapter relating how Sordo and his companions make their last stand is one of the clean, hard, sharp-focused jobs that Hemingway does at his best. The actual blowing of the bridge is as successful as the Burguete episode of *The Sun Also Rises.*

The testimony of the book points not to a decline but to the failure of new powers to develop. The long list of reasons why American novelists "peter out" after brilliant beginnings, which Hemingway compiled at the behest of the German admirer of poets in the first pages of *Green Hills of Africa*, contains nothing especially applicable to his own case. The fact is that he does not "peter out"—at least if this verb means to go on producing work of increasingly inferior quality. From the beginning he has been concerned less with the relations between human beings than with the relations between himself, or some projection of himself, and a harsh and mainly alien universe in which violence, suffering, and death are the rule, and which, in terms of what the human being expects of it, stubbornly refuses to make sense. *For Whom the Bell Tolls* cannot be said to enlarge this fundamental pattern.

Nor can the two fictions which Hemingway has written since, *Across the River and Into the Trees* and *The Old Man and the Sea:* he has elaborated variations upon his eternal themes, and the fact that the prose of the variations has at moments been the most satisfying written in his time does not alter the other fact that he remains limited to the battered but still combative hero, the "idyll," violence, sport, and the contemplation of courage.

The hero is no longer the man he once was; life has beaten him about; his strength and his illusions have waned. Colonel Cantrell in *Across the River* remembers the retreat from Caporetto; he is Tenente Frederic Henry, now fifty and with a bad heart. The old Cuban in *The Old Man and the Sea* is the disabled fighter, another Juan Belmonte able to go on killing bulls despite his fistula, another old boxer barely able to stay in the ring long enough to foul his man. Violence is now the matter of fantasies: on the last day of his life Cantrell's daydreams recall his fight with the two sailors; the old Cuban remembers playing "the hand game all night and all the next day with the big Negro." It still feels good to knock down ducks; it is still possible to love the quarry one kills; but now these feelings are possible because they revive memories.

Courage remains the one thing a man must have—courage

to face death by heart disease, courage to go on fighting the surges of a big fish. For Hemingway courage is a permanent element in a tragic formula: life is a trap in which a man is bound to be beaten and at last destroyed, but he emerges triumphant, in his full stature, if he manages to keep his chin up. What even the most devoted reader comes to object to in this is that the formula *is* a formula. He becomes somewhat sated by the subject. Most men have a certain amount of courage and the right to hope that when they are most in need it will not desert them; that they sometimes do not have it in such moments is a circumstance they may not be able to control. Jordan's worries about how he would behave, and his subsequent behavior, were wonderful; Colonel Cantrell's ability to face the fact of heart disease is all right; the Cuban's persistence in holding a fishline, and in beating off sharks with his tiller handle, is so familiar it skirts parody.

Similarly, as Hemingway and his heroes grow older, the eternal "idyll" moves us less. There is no doubt at all that *A Farewell to Arms* was that rarest of modern successes, a completely serious and successful love story. But the seismic affair with Maria in the sleeping-bag wears most of the same lineaments—the intense and more or less unexpected passion for a simple, unperfumed, ardent, mentally inert young woman, in circumstances such that the affair is the more poignant for being of such short duration. Robert Jordan has to die directly and love is the sweeter for having to be swallowed up in death. Cantrell has to die directly, also, and at fifty finds it appropriate to spend his last hours in a love affair with a girl of nineteen; for him, as for Hemingway, idylls are really important.

All through his work, from the short story where the owl goes flapping off through the forest to *Across the River and Into the Trees*, in which at one point a large and previously unperceived bird suddenly quits the lovers' gondola, Hemingway has sustained his effort to write well about the erotic. It is doubtless natural that the poet of the inarticulate should be bewitched by the problem of handling the emotional obbligati of the act in which humans are the least dependent upon words. In any case, sex combines automatically, in Hemingway's work, with sport and violence; the hunter of *Green Hills of Africa* kills an animal and then wants a woman; the young *contessa* shares Cantrell's attention with soldiering and the shooting of ducks. As Edmund Wilson has noted, love is merely one of the gratifications of the hero, and never a two-way enterprise. The women are submissive instruments, *figlie*, rabbits (it is curious how the pet names of the inamorata suggest prostitution). They exist, apparently, because the hero must experience his idyll. This, too, is formulary. And one feels that here again Hemingway's personal obsessions intrude upon—force their way into—the story in such a way that something does not seem entirely "hard and clean and true." Personality and the basic discipline are at odds.

My reasons for liking *The Old Man and the Sea* should perhaps take the form of a personal note, since it is not clear that all of them are entirely relevant to literary criticism. I do not think, however, that I am alone in holding them: in a country where seven million people buy fishing licenses every year, a story of an epic fight with a great fish is likely to find a well-disposed audience. I was put off, as many were, by the tinny fanfare from *Life* which accompanied publication, and by the knowing tone of *Life's* editorial which told us all how we should feel about the great writer it was sponsoring; but even that was not enough to spoil the story itself.

In addition, many of us who grew up reading Hemingway and have had too much trouble, since, explaining to our juniors why we read him at all, wanted a story from him that would vindicate us by showing that he was just as good

now as he was, at least, when he wrote *For Whom the Bell
Tolls*. We wanted proof that *Across the River* was just an
aberration and not the beginning of a decline. In other
words, we wanted Hemingway to come through with a good
book for the same reason that, when we read the book, we
wanted old Santiago to get his big marlin back to the shore.

What we got was this defiantly simple story of a simple
man and his simple but great courage and his simple greatness in defeat, which is also an impressive account of what
it must be like to get mixed up with a fish too powerful for
one's equipment. (I trust that *The Old Man and the Sea*
is not an allegory about the Writer, his Art, and the Critic-
sharks; and I respect Hemingway too much to believe that
it is.) The prose read like Hemingway as we remembered
him; it was prose that no one else could have written. In
other words we got, within limits, what we had been wanting.

The trouble was that after the first pleasure the awareness of those limits began to set in. The task Hemingway
had set himself, after all, was not a very large one. This was
a long short-story, not a novel, and as such had less sub-
stance, perhaps, than a story like "The Snows of Kiliman-
jaro." It had the qualities we have always admired in
Hemingway—the concreteness, the sensuous awareness, the
spareness of his best prose. One could also assert—and some
did—that *The Old Man and the Sea* attained an almost
mythic stature, with old Santiago becoming something of an
archetypal figure of Man Bereft of All but Courage; but this,
after all, seemed too much of a burden for old Santiago to
carry. In the last accounting, *The Old Man and the Sea* is an
excellent Hemingway piece, worthy of the writer of "Big
Two-Hearted River," but like this story a tale of modest
dimensions about catching fish. It is not, by far, the novel
we hope Hemingway will yet give us.

Thus, finally, one has to concede that William Faulkner

was right, in his famous newspaper interview, to put Hemingway behind Thomas Wolfe and himself. Hemingway has, in fact, devoted his great talent to relatively small subjects. There was a moment, the moment of *For Whom the Bell Tolls,* when one could talk about Hemingway's growth. In his early work his interest in violence had been largely aesthetic, although the gap between aesthetics and ethics was bridged to some extent by his insistence that integrity is an element of aesthetics. On the other hand, a forceful moral conviction puts Robert Jordan in the predicament of *For Whom the Bell Tolls;* he dies because his conscience has told him that the way of violence is the way which a decent human must take. Violence thus occupies a new place in the scheme of values. For four days which are almost isolated from the rest of time we live beside Jordan. His destiny will not wait. We live with him in the dramatic present, joining him at his crisis and seeing him through it; he faces destruction with a certain dignity and decorum. The technical failures of the book come from Hemingway's not having faced the formal requirement of the "novel of destiny" that it shall not delay, dally, digress, that the reader must feel the progress of the action as rectilinear. But, quite apart from this kind of defect, one admired *For Whom the Bell Tolls* because its violence possessed so much meaning. The subject, in Faulkner's sense, had size. But the subjects Hemingway has treated since do not have size. For the greatest satisfaction one must reread his early work. It should be added, in simple justice, that this satisfaction remains very great indeed.

10

The Menace of the Paperback

One of the pleasanter things about literary conferences is that they bring you a lot of mail. Coming in the off season, they get space in the papers and time on the radio. Your friends, who doubtless were on the point of writing to'you anyway, read or hear what you say or are alleged to have said, and immediately take their pens in hand. So do a number who make it very clear that they would do themselves violence if they ever suspected anyone of thinking them your friends. What these people say is interesting, too, and they are frequently even more poisonously frank than your friends. But the friends are frank enough!

Among my best ones is an editor for a large publisher—both of whom had better be kept anonymous here, for reasons that will be clear before the end of this paragraph. At the very moment when our conference* was raking over the whole subject of the future of the novel, my friend was beginning to wonder if the novel, not to speak of its having a future, even had a present. He had just received, it appears, the final part of a long-awaited manuscript. He wrote:

Instead of running the 40,000 words we expected it ran far over a hundred thousand and the total length is about a quarter of a million words. Handled in the ordinary way it would give us a loss of two cents a copy on an edition of 5,000 if we charged

*Conference on the Contemporary Novel, Harvard, August 3-5, 1953.

199

$4.50. At $4.50 we doubt that we could sell five thousand. So where are we? At $3.95 we would lose well over a quarter a copy and sell more. . . . Maybe the problems of the novel you were discussing at Cambridge will be settled by the economic extinction of the novel.

Well, perhaps that is the way it will all end, although my friend adds that his is "probably too simple a statement and probably not true anyway." But on the same day that I read his letter, one of the literary gossip columns reported that the entire first printing of the paperback edition of James Jones's *From Here to Eternity*, a cool half-million copies, had sold out in one brief week. And at three times the price of ordinary paperback fiction.

And there you have it: the novel may be, and probably is, in parlous straits, but if the paperback novel is in any danger of extinction, money has simply lost its familiar voice. Or, in other words, the economics of publishing are right now in a way to change the nature of the novel.

The paperback on the table beside my typewriter has three pictures on the cover: one of a drunk sprawling across a bar, one of a newspaper office with a man telephoning and a girl waiting to hand him some presumably important papers, and one of a man sitting in what seems to be a night club with a lewd-looking floozy lounging on his knee and a pair of unmistakable thugs lolling in the background. I didn't buy the book because of the pictures. But the fact remains that the pictures didn't keep me from buying the book. I bought it in a cigar store at ten in the evening. I had just finished a job of work and gone out for a cup of coffee. It was too late to start a new job, too early to go to bed. What I needed was two hours of the kind of entertainment that would keep me occupied until bedtime and then not keep me awake. I got it for the price of a package of cigarettes—and thereby identified myself as one of the sixty million

whom the paperback manufacturers count on for their
market.

To make the record complete, the title is *Come, Fill the
Cup*. Author: Harlan Ware. The story went through two
printings under the Random House imprint, was an "alter-
nate selection" of one of the book clubs, and finally went
into paper covers early in 1953. You may never have heard
of Harlan Ware, but as the story unwinds you are sure to
get at least a vague feeling that you have read *Come, Fill
the Cup*. Or else that you read a review of it. Or just possibly
that some bore cornered you at a party and told you about it
at great length. And the chances are that you are wrong.
You have merely been reading average-run paperbacks.
What gives you that feeling of having been here before is
that Harlan Ware is a purveyor of gimmicks, and the gimmick at this writing is the stock-in-trade of the paperback
novel.

In the present context, the gimmick is any special device,
unique twist, or peculiar slant that can be worked into a
fiction to spice it up. Gimmicks can be connected with background, plot, characterization, psychological notation, or
almost any other aspect of fiction. Even the technique of the
Jamesian "point of view" can become a gimmick, according
to the use to which it is put. Sex, of course, is an abundant
source of potential gimmicks, but it would be a horrendous
mistake to think that it had anything like an exclusive
monopoly.

Any real paperback can be depended on to turn up one
or more gimmicks, just as surely as its cover can be depended upon to turn up new evidence that woman is a
mammal. *Come, Fill the Cup* has several very fine ones. The
hero is a reformed rummy, but not so reformed that his
need for a drink doesn't have to be fought off whenever the
action slows down a bit. As a rummy he is automatically

interesting, because alcoholism is so much a problem of our time that even the most abstemious of us can easily—or uneasily—imagine himself filling a seat at a meeting of Alcoholics Anonymous. The story is told from his point of view. Will he, won't he, weaken and take a drink? It's a gimmick.

There is a gimmick in the situation also. The background of the story is a metropolitan newspaper. Now 160 million living Americans, minus perhaps a few newspaper people, consider newspaper life unusually glamorous, and this background has been used so often before that it can hardly in itself be considered one of the special slants of *Come, Fill the Cup*. But get this: the hero is an editor and has to deal with a wealthy and capricious owner who keeps sending him on errands in no way connected with the operation of a newspaper but calculated to make any editor, ex-alcoholic or not, turn to strong drink with a loud sigh.

The owner gives his reformed drunk of an editor the unwelcome job of rehabilitating an extremely unreformed young drunk of a Princeton graduate who has an affinity for picturesque alcoholic adventure—the ex-blind leading the blind, so to speak. The young sot has about as much sense of responsibility as one of Steinbeck's *paisanos*. His taste for adventure gets an innocent man killed and involves him in both girl-trouble and a feud with some fairly slimy figures from the Chicago underworld. Consequently the editor-hero has to fight racketeers in order to rescue his charge. And each victory gives him another exclusive story for his paper. There is thus a large gimmick in the plot.

The story also has the Modern Psychology gimmick. The young man drinks because his incredibly idiotic mother has nauseated him since babyhood with the wrong kind of affection. His name is Boyd; she calls him "Boydie"—and in this day when the Bronx has spread halfway across the country the pet name is almost a small gimmick in itself. But let that one pass. His drinking is an act of revolt against a parent who hasn't read Gesell; that is gimmick enough.

In spite of this impressive array, however, *Come, Fill the Cup* is on the restrained side as far as the accumulation of gimmicks is concerned. Many of the standard sources are neglected. The treatment of sex, for instance, is perfectly straight. The one-time city-room girl who has left the paper to marry the young drunk eventually gets sick of all the horseplay and divorces him; she nearly marries the old drunk (who loved her long before his own, now liquor-broken, marriage) but changes her mind and remarries her ex-husband when, at the end of the story, he straightens out and comes off the bottle. The only other female in the story, of an age to misbehave, is a gangster's whore from south of the border, but she stays more or less chastely in the role of the woman men squabble over. Unless I have missed something, everyone in the book has normal instincts.

Violence is also treated without introducing variations from the norm. There is some shooting. Fists fly now and then. A Negro is blown into the next world by a pineapple attached to the starter of a car. A pair of cops manhandle a thug, but not very seriously. No sadism; no masochism.

Only the regular reader of the paperbacks can realize, as a matter of fact, how many opportunities *Come, Fill the Cup* lets slip by. For the average paperback has developed the possibilities of the gimmick to a remarkable degree. The background regularly shows the reader a slice of unfamiliar life: the vice-den, the fairy-roost, the esoteric worlds of the circus, ballet, theater, opera, and so on. The casts of characters contain enough eccentrics of one kind and another to populate a casebook of practical anthropology. Standard treatment of sex involves behavior that could document the Kinsey "report": heroines whose favorite loveplay consists of being beaten, heroes with epic sexual appetites, subsidiary characters who are overt lesbians and homosexuals. And the violence that is epidemic in such fiction is no longer the slam-bang bitter bloodshed of twenty years ago; it is cruel and, more often than not, perverse—the violence of the comic books made more explicit and convincing for the consumption of adults. Gimmicks wear out fast. The time when the author could count on keeping his reader attentive merely by making his characters violate all ten Commandments is evidently past; the need for hotter stuff is constant.

The popularity of the gimmick has even changed the nature of our detective fiction. The old-fashioned "mystery," dependent for its interest and charm on offering the reader a problem to unravel, if he could, before the detective reached his solution, is well along on the way out. The problem itself takes a subordinate position, while the chief interest comes from the presence of an assortment of curious fauna displayed against an esoteric backdrop. In the last detective yarn—if that is what it is—that I have happened to pick up, the lady who gets killed is, in addition to being a *prima ballerina,* a rampant lesbian; her husband is a dope addict; the muscle-bound male star devotes his spare time to the predatory pursuit of the rest of the troupe, preferring masculine to feminine companions but excluding neither sex completely; the hero and heroine, afflicted by nothing more than mild nymphomania and complete lack of inhibition, end by seeming somewhat dull in comparison. Meanwhile, the murderer turns out to be a choreographer, also homosexual, who kills because he is afraid someone will reveal his Communist past. But by the time the identity of the killer becomes clear we no longer care. The murder is simply lost among all the gimmicks.

The gimmick novel bids fair to be the novel of the future. Paperback publishing is big business, and one of the immutable laws of big business says that any investment had better show some kind of return. The paperback people count on low distribution costs (using the same system of distribution magazines have used for years), low unit costs, and mass sales. They do not take the risks of the hard-cover publishers; they have a good idea of how well a book is likely to go over before they set the presses rolling. But the possibility of a book's laying a five-million-copy egg is still not one that they can contemplate with equanimity. They need sure-fire successes, well-tried stuff.

Meanwhile, rising production costs have put the regular trade edition publishers, who are the people who do the real gambling on the unknown commodities, in a position where they stand to make little from the sales of their own editions. The "break-even" level has mounted so high that if they want to stay in business they are forced to keep an eye on the tastes of the book clubs, movies, and reprint publishers. No trade edition house, however high its standards, can afford to sniff at manuscripts likely to attract the reprint trade. They, too, need a certain amount of sure fire. The pressure is on them, too.

It is also on the novelists themselves. Not all of the latter are as frank as Hemingway was when he remarked that he wrote *For Whom the Bell Tolls* with Gary Cooper in mind, but few of them display any marked lack of interest in the size of the cash return—and those who do are not necessarily the best. By and large, 'novelists have always been docile in accepting the conditions of their time. Some few resist; the others go along.

So with trade publishers, reprint publishers, and authors all in a way to profit by its success, the gimmick novel runs a good chance of being with us for a long time.

Thus it is now time for certain literary critics to start up the old dirge, to the effect that the novel is dying, the novel is dead, or even that the novel is already in the ground.

And they will know precisely what killed it, just as they have known what has killed the novel, at regular intervals, for the last century. Actually there is no more reason to lament the demise of the novel now than there has ever been. The novel has changed its nature before. It will doubtless, under the influence of the paperback, change it again. Critics seem to have a singular inability to distinguish between mutation and mortality.

Ortega y Gasset's famous argument, in his *Notes on the Novel*, is an excellent sample of what such critics can do. Ortega could convince any reader who understood the word novel to mean what Ortega understood it to mean. He had in mind fictions which have just enough action to satisfy the psychological needs of the reader who must have something to focus his mind on, which are full of atmosphere and abound in "the rich texture of life," which absorb us so completely that we become "provincials in the country of the author," and which delve deeply into human motive. His contention that this novel was disappearing was not hard to accept—subjects, *données*, and situations appropriate to it do seem to become fewer as time goes on. Certainly the supply is not inexhaustible. But Ortega's notion of the novel was based on the works of his favorites, i.e., Stendhal, Dostoevski, and Proust. Since the writing of his *Notes* we have had novels from France, Italy, and the United States which are full of action, handle the question of motive by recourse to psychologies of obsession (a rapid process), can hardly be said to "provincialize" us, and convey blessed little feeling of life's rich texture. Ortega was right as far as he went, but he went little farther than saying that the novel cannot and does not repeat itself. He simply failed to see that the novel is capable of almost infinite self-renewal.

The novel may, at this moment, be renewing itself through the use of the gimmick. By our prevailing standards the behavior of the present common run of paperbacks prevents them from being first-rate. We want backgrounds that offer more than strangeness, human behavior that appeals to something other than our more perverse curiosities, characters who have significance in truly human terms, and action attractive for other things than its mere rapidity.

But prevailing standards have a way of ceasing to prevail. We tolerate swift action, these days, so long as we are not made too thoroughly aware of the devices the novelist uses to attain it. We applaud plausible dialogue—and the author of the most ephemeral cigar-store novel knows more about this subject than even the most gifted knew forty years ago. No one objects to the kind of elliptical narration that the novelists have learned from the movies. The development of a conventional interior monologue, used as a device not only for clarifying motive but also for explaining action and for foreshadowing, is generally accepted. And we have even come to expect the novelist to be conversant with at least the vulgarized versions of the discoveries which, since 1900, have greatly changed our notions about the composition of the human personality and even about the workings of the human mind. No longer ago than 1930-35 these procedures were gimmicks, as everyone knows who remembers the literary beginnings of writers like James M. Cain.

Much of our current highbrow distaste for the gimmick novel rises from resentment at being exploited. We have a feeling that the author's proficiency in many branches of his craft is being used exclusively to manipulate us. We dislike the cynicism this implies. We insist upon seriousness, and from our point of view such behavior is not completely serious, especially when the tricks are so blatantly obvious.

But suppose that here and there some writer manages to use the techniques now common to the paperback, and all of its characteristic materials, *without* outraging our taste for seriousness. For this is precisely what is bound to happen. Either we will become so inured to gimmickry that we will no longer be aware of gimmicks as such, or they will be smoothly enough handled so that we will not feel exploited. Nothing inherent in the conventions of the paperback novel need, in the long run, prevent its reaching the highest level of quality. Not many will attain that level—but not many attained greatness in the days before the paperback was invented. Admittedly a first glance at the paperbacks makes the future of the novel look dark, but the future of the novel almost always looks dark anyhow. Nothing is more dangerous than to proclaim that the novel is dead, because the corpse has a nastily inconvenient way of climbing back on its feet again.

The future of the novel never looked darker anywhere than it did just about a hundred years ago in France. A stupendous amount of fiction was being published. The new literacy that had followed upon the establishment of democratic institutions had produced a public with money to spend and leisure for reading. The industrial revolution had brought cheaper paper and abundant printer's ink; the steam printing press developed into a high-production machine. Someone had even had the luminous idea that no law of nature requires a publisher to sell an expensive binding with every book he puts out. And Emile de Girardin, in the process of inventing the modern newspaper, had discovered that any continued story, so long as each instalment ended at a sufficiently high point in the action, helped circulation immensely. Fiction prospered, at least as to quantity, but its quality—leaving room for certain remarkable exceptions which seem to have been invisible at the time—fell to a record low.

For the public that was buying the newspapers and books had not been brought up on the good classical tradition. It lacked taste. It asked only to be interested and amused, and it would accept whatever interested and amused it. Aside from the elder Dumas and Eugene Sue, we hardly remember the names of those who catered to the taste for what most of the time was nothing but horrid trash.

One of the finest generations of critics the world has ever known—men like Jules Janin, Gustave Planche, and the great Sainte-Beuve—complained, roared, snarled, and snubbed. But the thunder from Parnassus had no visible effect; the spate of fiction rolled on regardless, while the critics raised the cry, Where is the good old novel of tradition? They seem to have meant the romance in the manner of Walter Scott, who had been popular in their youth, and the realistic, episodic novel of Le Sage. But whatever they meant, they did not find it, and they forthwith concluded that the day of the novel was gone.

Yet of course those years from 1828 to 1857 saw the birth of the modern French novel. Lengthen the period by a decade, to make it include the beginnings of French naturalism, and it would be impossible to find another that produced so many excellent novelists: Balzac, Stendhal and Flaubert, Champfleury and the minor realists, Feydeau and Feuillet, those predecessors of Henry James and Paul Bourget, as well as the young Goncourt brothers and the young Zola.

Where was the novel? It was where the great critics were not looking for it. Sainte-Beuve could not abide the cheap coarseness of Balzac. To Stendhal he preferred the novels of Scott, Manzoni, and the author of the monumentally insipid *Voyage Around My Room*, Xavier de Maistre. He did better in perceiving the worth of Flaubert, for he was older when *Madame Bovary* appeared and was not insensitive to the new spirit of the times; but still, as his detractors love to tell us, he hardly gave *Madame Bovary* its due. His record, as a judge of fiction, was not good. Nor was that of most of his critical contemporaries any better. The story of how gradually French critics became aware that Balzac, Stendhal, and Flaubert had changed the nature of the French novel has not been told in its entirety, even yet. But this much is clear: for a space the critics were at least a quarter-century behind their time. To most of them Balzac was merely a rather noisy fortune-seeker who alienated so many that at length the only voice raised in his behalf was his own; Baudelaire and Taine were doing something that marked the beginning of a new day when they spoke out in favor of his work. For the common run of critics his fictions were too unlike those they knew and admired; his novels bawled and squalled, and their similarities to those of Eugène Sue (look at characters like Vautrin) were all too obvious. Flaubert, likewise, had to be discovered by a generation much younger than his own. And Stendhal's great fame is the work of the twentieth century, not the nineteenth.

Doubtless it was because these French critics were blinded by prejudice that they failed in part to detect the presence of great writers. They had been reared in an aristocratic tradition, and the novel was not aristocratic. And then it was also true that winnowing out the excellent from the mediocre was a discouraging task: there was just too much fiction. But it is true at the same time that one of the reasons for their failure was that they were simply unable to discriminate the good from the poor when they had the chance.

The situation in America a hundred years later is not greatly different. We have the same flood of fiction, the same appeal to a new and untrained audience, the same incentives for author and publisher to turn out fifth-rate novels. Nothing proves that there is, or will be, the same proportion of good stuff among the other, but we had better assume that there is, or will be. For the novel has always tended to heed public

demand. Dostoevski and Dickens, we have to remember,
gave the public what no public has the right to expect, but
in the process they also gave it what it asked for. If the
paperback does not develop into the novel of the future,
what can the novel of the future possibly be?

So long as the public reads, there is every reason to hope:
eventually the paperback will absorb, so to speak, its own
gimmicks. This seems almost inevitable. But the paperback
still remains a menace for all that. Not to the novel, but to
the critics. For the conditions of the paperback's success offer
the critics the same opportunity to miss the presence of
greatness that was offered the French critics of a century
ago. In any circumstances, the odds would be against the
critics. And the present circumstances in which American
critics do their work make failure doubly likely. For it is the
mode of the moment for our critics to behave like those
figures in Dante's *Inferno,* who are punished by having their
heads twisted about on their bodies so that they can see
nowhere but behind them.

For some time, American critics have been staring resolutely into the past. If they want to see what is happening
now, or get some inkling of what is going to happen, they
would do much better to turn their heads in almost any
other direction.

11

James Agee

the question of wasted talent

To the dozen or so good reasons that have been suggested for our having no new major novelists in America I should like to add one more. America now maintains so many areas in which a creative talent can find room for exercise that a writer whose gifts at one time would have assured us a long series of good fictions is now invited to divert his energies in a dozen different directions. And for an example of what happens to solicit some talents I would offer the case of James Agee, who had a great gift and would, one suspects, have written some fine novels.

Agee died in 1955 of coronary occlusion at the age of forty-five, leaving one book of poems, *Permit Me Voyage;* one book about sharecropping, *Let Us Now Praise Famous Men;* one short novel, *The Morning Watch;* and the manuscript of a longer novel, *A Death in the Family.* If you knew anything else of his, it was because you had come upon a fugitive piece in some magazine or other, or had happened to notice his name in connection with the script of a movie. The truth is that on paper Agee's accomplishments are quickly listed and seem only mildly impressive.

When *Permit Me Voyage* was published (1934), in the "Yale Series of Younger Poets," Agee was shortly out of college and earning his living as a writer on *Fortune;* and the two main lines that his life as a writer would take were

212

already evident. The book revealed a kind of agonized self-searcher who would go on for the rest of his life trying to put his feelings about himself and the world into some acceptable order. His work on *Fortune* revealed a craftsman who could lose himself, with complete detachment, in any ephemeral piece of writing which happened to challenge his skill. (It was clear that he could, at least temporarily, lose his troubles in it also.) The self-searching would go on in his poems, in his study of sharecroppers, and toward the last of his life in what little fiction he had time left to write. The craftsman wrote articles for *Fortune*, *Time*, and *Life*, movie reviews for the *Nation*, and the movie scripts he published as well as those which were filmed in Hollywood. What may be harder to believe is that both lines of activity were so important to him.

The poems in *Permit Me Voyage* were a selection from early work that Agee thought worth saving. Some were overly intricate, some precious, some extremely good and mature work. Reviewers deprecated the preciousness (one remarked that the title itself is a circumlocution for "gangway") and admired the poet's musical ear. They also talked, more often than not unfavorably, about the book's curious dedication. Actually it was the "Dedication"—in quotes because it is the title of a section of the book—which most clearly revealed the direction in which Agee's career was likely to go.

Most dedications are one line long, on a special page. Agee's "Dedication" ran from page 16 on to page 23. It starts by offering the book to God, and to Agee's friends, and relatives, and teachers; it then enumerates men he has admired without knowing them, like Chaplin and Joyce, and offers the book to them; it continues with an offering to all those "who have told the truth," and from them goes on to men he disagrees with or disapproves of, or even hates, including

8

the then current enemies of humanity. At the very end it calls down a blessing upon all:

Have mercy upon us therefore, O deep God of the Void, spare this race in this your earth still in our free choice: who will turn to you and again fail you, and once more turn as ever we have done. And make the eyes of our hearts, and the voice of our hearts in speech, honest and lovely within the fences of our nature, and a little clear.

This was an embarrassing text to find in the middle of a book of poetry. By no standard was it poetry, but rather a sort of declamatory prose; and in a way it seemed to be, and was, a wilful parade of eccentricity. Unfriendly readers had much fun with it. Friendly ones were likely to pass it off as a slip for which the quality of the rest of the book more than atoned. But as one looks back at it now, knowing what Agee was going to write later, it appears as a first systematic effort to straighten out the conflicts, and particularly the conflicting loyalties, of his own life. For his loyalties were paradoxical: his Tennessee blood and his Exeter-Harvard education, his conservatively Episcopalian bringing-up and his leftist political sympathies, his great appreciation of "cultural advantages" and his sense of guilt at enjoying privilege, his devotion to experimental art and his deep suspicion of the phony. The prayer for clarity of vision and speech, at the end of the "Dedication," announced much less the dedication of the poems than the dedication of the poet. Meanwhile his book got him known as a young poet of promise, at a moment in his life when writing poetry, as a regular activity, was already behind him.

He had been born in Knoxville and his father, who died in Agee's childhood, had been from the hills. Yet Agee was hardly the Mountain White some of his friends liked to think him. His mother's family was from the North, and a grandmother was among the first woman M.A.'s at one of the large middle western universities. He was raised in Knoxville and, after his father's death, at Saint Andrew's School, near Sewanee and the University of the South; at fourteen he was sent to Philips Exeter. His mother had remarried and later moved to Maine, and Agee did not see the South again, even as a quick visitor, until several years after he had finished college. Much as he liked to think of himself as "hill-born" in Thomas Wolfe's sense, he moved north too early in life and acclimated himself too thoroughly to go down as a version of Wolfe's alien and unreconstructed hero. By preference he spent his vacations in New York.

At Exeter, once he got over the uneasiness and homesickness of his first year, his career had been normal. He was awkward and poorly co-ordinated, but sheer strength and physical endurance got him on the track and swimming teams; he edited the literary magazine, mixed in musical activities, and joined a fraternity. He also wrote, mostly poetry and short stories: "Ann Garner," the long narrative in the *Permit Me Voyage* collection, was first printed in the *Exeter Monthly*. In classwork he was at least good enough to get into Harvard without difficulty.

During his first year at Harvard, Lincoln Kirstein's *Hound and Horn* reprinted "Ann Garner," and Alfred Kreymborg listed Agee in *Our Singing Strength* as one of the young poets who had read too deeply in T. S. Eliot. Actually Agee had not read Eliot until after leaving Exeter, but Kreymborg's sensing, on the strength of the one poem of Agee's that he could then have read, the presence of an unusual talent, testifies to his critical acumen. Agee went through Harvard, writing constantly for the *Advocate*, winning prizes for translations from Latin and for his own poetry, singing in the glee club, and making durable friendships. Except in physical science, in which he was nothing if not inept, he was a better than passable student. He edited the *Advocate*

in his senior year and, possibly because the annual parody
number that year was a particularly telling take-off of *Time*,
was offered a job in Henry Luce's establishment upon
graduation.

Agee had no illusions as to what was expected of him
as a writer for *Fortune:* he was supposed to take an assignment and turn the material he and his researcher could
gather into a sufficiently slick and smooth-running story.
There was no doubting his sincerity when he said that he
was working "in a whorehouse," but there was also no doubt
that he took great satisfaction in concocting, out of the most
recalcitrant technical materials, what have to be called
masterpieces of that kind of journalism.

His ability to plunge so deeply into a *Fortune* assignment
was the first manifestation of what it was in Agee that has
since made people say he did not keep his "promise." Con-
ventionally, if one writes a book of poems which "show
promise" then one must go on and write another book of
poems or the promise is not "kept." But Agee lacked, even
more than other writers of our time, the traditional respect
for genres. He went one step beyond Baudelaire's notion
that any work of art contains an obstacle which the artist
creates as part of the act of conceiving what he is going to
do, and then conquers in the execution. For Agee, if not in
theory at least in his practice of writing, the presence of an
obstacle, in any kind of writing job whatever, was enough
to give the job the status of a work of art. It would be false,
of course, to say that he set as high a value on a *Fortune*
article as on a poem or a piece of fiction, but it is gospel true
that he could lose himself as completely in writing of one
kind as in writing of the others. What counted was the job,
the problem that was presented to the craftsman.

Admittedly, Agee was an extreme case—but just how
much American talent is diverted in this way from the tradi-

tional literary forms? And how many novels have gone un-
written in our time because writers have satisfied the urge-
to-write by writing which we do not label literary?

In any case, by 1934 his poetry had become a rather
desultory pursuit. Agee had always been superbly indifferent
about what happened to finished manuscripts. (Still further
evidence that for him the important part of any writing job
was the doing.) He kept no records. A piano bench in his
apartment was overflowing with manuscript, but he told
one New York publisher that he did not have the material
for a second book of poems. Occasionally a piece of his verse
would appear in a magazine like the *New Masses* or the
Partisan Review, and doubtless still other pieces appeared
in periodicals where no one has yet thought of looking for
them. Compiling a check list of his poems becomes, for this
reason, as difficult a task as one could take on. Manuscripts
of a long "Don Juan," a satire on his youth and education,
and of a long poem called "Pygmalion," which a dozen
people remember having seen at one time or another, seem
never to have got into print. The same is true of a novel,
"The Circle," which he had written at, off and on, since he
was at Exeter, and a series of parodies of radio broadcasts
to which, at one point, he devoted considerable time. So long
as he stayed with *Fortune* the process of scattering went on.

Fortunately, an assignment to an article on the life of
typical sharecroppers sent Agee back to the South in 1936
and opened the way to a new round of self-examination.
Walker Evans, a photographer known for the puritanical
severity of his work, was assigned to the sharecropper topic
along with Agee. The two overstayed their time in rural
Alabama and brought back to New York a pile of text and
photographs which belonged legally to *Fortune* but which
Fortune, for reasons which the editors were not obliged to
make public, decided not to use. It took Agee and Evans

a year to get a release of their material, work it over into a book, and take the book to a publisher.

By the time Houghton Mifflin brought out the volume, it was 1941. For bad timing, a book on sharecropping in 1941 probably sets some kind of record. Writers like Erskine Caldwell had been working that side of the street for years. The poor white, like the Okies and Arkies of Steinbeck, had already hardened into a fixed image in the popular mind. Events like the 1939 Hitler-Stalin pact had thrown our attitudes toward local social problems into a nameless confusion. And we were only months away from war. *Let Us Now Praise Famous Men* was probably a poor title anyhow, one hardly calculated to attract readers. According to one report, the book sold fewer than six hundred copies before it was remaindered.

Yet Lionel Trilling called this book "the most realistic and the most important moral effort of our American generation," and he was right. Agee had come upon one of those facts which create, when the individual confronts them, profound emotional disturbance. He had always known about the wretchedness of the tenant farmers of the Central South and had taken the appropriate liberal attitudes toward their predicament, but now he had been thrust up against the human reality of sharecropping and felt called, impelled, obsessively driven to tell about it. At the end of the "Dedication" in *Permit Me Voyage* he had prayed for the clear vision and the clear voice. Now was the time to use them. That there had been other books about sharecroppers made no difference, because his real, deep subject was not the sharecroppers themselves; it was the emotional experience of meeting the fact of sharecroppers. For this subject, everything he had learned on *Fortune* and elsewhere about making prose do what he wanted, and everything he had learned about words from writing poetry, would barely be adequate.

Like most of his generation Agee had always had an immense scorn of the phony. More than most he distrusted himself, suspecting the phony in his own nature. This had been the implicit burden of the "Dedication" in *Permit Me Voyage;* more generally, everything he had ever written, with the exception of what he did for *Fortune* (wherein he could approach assigned subjects with complete objectivity), had reflected a similar self-doubt—a questioning not only of his own sincerity but also of the possibility of anyone's ever being completely sincere.

The problem, in other words, was one of telling the truth about what had been seen and felt by a man whom Agee distrusted—himself. To let the reader see the truth, he had to tell him enough about the man Agee so that the reader could at least guess how much the truth was being distorted in passing through the refracting apparatus of a temperament. This was a preoccupation, of course, with what Henry James called "point of view," and would have concerned Agee equally if he had been writing a novel instead of *Let Us Now Praise Famous Men.* But in this case the problem was more agonizing because the people Agee was writing about existed independently of him, and his obligation was deeper than, and different in kind from, a novelist's obligation to his characters. The truth about a character is what the novelist asserts to be the truth. The truth about the sharecroppers was what it was; the writer could only distort it at best. Thus this book—which is catalogued in my local library under Economics—became a covert autobiography.

At the same time, he wanted to honor the truth with the best prose he could write. This is a sample:

Huge thunderheads were barely lifted on the horizon, their convolutions a scarcely discernible brain-shape of silver in the strength of the light. They were no use; they were a trick a drought sun likes to play; and gets away with over and over

again. They ride up looking rich as doom, and darken; the look
of the earth is already dark purple, olivegreen and wealthy under
their shadow and the air goes cold and waits. They let loose drops
as big as teacups, about a dozen to the square rod, of which you
hear the palpable splash and break; and list off to one side. The
sun, which has meanwhile lowered a very little, shines again...

Agee hoped that people would read his book aloud. In
our time, such hopes are probably vain. But let the reader
now try mouthing lines like "the palpable splash and break,"
slowly enough to feel the consonants with his mouth muscles,
and then faster to get the rhythm: this is prose meant to
register through two or three senses at once. It may be out
of place in a book catalogued under Economics, but it is
excellent prose for translating an emotion. Agee could be as
suspicious as he liked of the artist in himself; still it would
have been as false to have suppressed the artist as to have
let the artist distort and artify the experience.

He had conceived *Let Us Now Praise Famous Men* as the
opening book of a much longer job, probably in three volumes, to be called "Three Tenant Families." So far as I
know, the rest of it was never finished. One suspects why:
the longer work would have had to be a more thoroughly
"objective" piece of reporting, and this was not what Agee
was interested in. His essential work was done when he
had finished with his own emotions.

Doubtless he had other reasons also for not continuing.
Between 1936 and 1941 his attitudes changed considerably.
At Harvard he had not been much aware of living in a social
revolution. *Fortune,* on the other hand, had been a school for
militant liberals. His sense of being his brother's keeper took
him to the Left—and he went that way with his usual violent
thoroughness, taking the religion of his childhood along with
him. Early in *Let Us Now Praise Famous Men* he called
himself "a communist and a catholic." Before the book went

to press he added a note saying that he had given up being either. Actually, all that he gave up was the names, not his intense social responsibility and not, I am sure, his faith. But he had been disillusioned about institutions of all kinds, and in 1941 felt in a way much lonelier than when he had begun his book. This single fact could have kept him from going on with the larger project.

And in addition, during the years before *Let Us Now Praise Famous Men* was published, he had discovered the possibilities of the movie script. From childhood he had been an abandoned movie-goer, capable of watching the same film with unremitting attention a dozen times. He had trained on the old silent film, with actors like Emil Jannings and directors like King Vidor. Gradually he had come to see the script itself as a kind of literary form, and one which will permit a writer to do what he cannot do in other forms. The ordinary movie script is dialogue plus some directions—not much more. Agee's notion of a script, on the other hand, was that it should be a work of imagination unhampered by the material limitations under which even the best directors have to work. It should set up, in the most minute detail, the ideal—different for every film—of what the director should try to approximate.

The implications of such a notion become clear from an examination of a sample script which Agee printed in the short-lived review, *Films*, in 1939. He had been attracted by the possibilities of André Malraux's *Man's Fate*. Critics are fond of pointing to one brilliant scene in this novel, in which the heroes, having been captured by the Chinese National-ists, prepare for execution. The men lie in the recreation space of an old school which has been turned into a prison, waiting to be taken out and pushed into the boiler of a locomotive. One of them gulps a cyanide pellet. The other gives away his cyanide to a fellow-prisoner who has lost his

nerve and then walks out with the guard, toward his death.
The scene is regularly cited as evidence that Malraux has a
"cinematographic" imagination.

To produce for the screen the emotion Malraux gets on
the printed page, Agee's script goes far beyond the novel;
it intensifies detail, builds rhythms by the movements of the
lens, blends sound and light effect and image. Explicit speci-
fication of the effects goes so far as to prescribe the kind of
rawness of tone known in newsreels before the development
of panchromatic film. Emphases have to be changed: in the
novel, when the pellet of poison is dropped in passing from
one maimed hand to another and has to be groped for along
the ground in the dark, one sees nothing; in Agee's script a
hand recovers it and holds it in the light, toward the lens,
"like a jewel."

Such work could occupy, and completely satisfy, Agee's
imagination: it was of the same nature as the work on
Fortune, in that what it offered was problems to be solved
without self-involvement. I am not sure how many scripts
Agee did between 1937 and World War II. At least one
other, "The House," was published in *New Letters in
America*. Later he joined with a photographer, Helen Leavitt,
to write and make the documentary of Harlem called *The
Quiet One*, which circulates still among film clubs and stu-
dents of movie potentials. When finally he went to Hollywood to write scripts for John Huston, he went not as a
hack looking for a job but as a practitioner of a special art;
the relationship was like that of a writer looking for a
publisher.

But Hollywood came later. Agee was 4-F in the draft
and spent the war working for *Time*, writing much ephemeral stuff but also doing things like the "cover stories" of
the death of President Roosevelt and the dropping of the
Hiroshima bomb. A man who cared about what happened to

what he wrote would have been unhappy. No one would have called Agee spectacularly happy; he had as much difficulty keeping his life in order as most of us do. But it is doubtful that the anonymity and short life of what he wrote contributed to his discomfort. Nor, on the other hand, did he consider his stuff trash. One of his rare prides was inspired by the long, unsigned review he did for *Time* of *The Iceman Cometh*.

He also took over the movie column of the *Nation* at that last fine moment in the *Nation's* history when Diana Trilling was writing about fiction, Joseph Wood Krutch covering the plays, and Randall Jarrell reviewing current poetry. The editors put no restrictions on him except that he turn in his copy on time. His reviews were not really reports on current entertainment. His eye was on what a movie had done, even accidentally, that had not been done—or done so well—before, and widely open to spot missed opportunities for greatness. As always, his prose was turned into an instrument for a special purpose. The story that when seeing so many movies became too great a drain on Agee's time, the editors of the *Nation* invited him to go on writing about movies whether he saw them or not—they liked to print prose of such quality—is probably apocryphal, but must have been started by someone who knew prose of quality when he saw it.

In Hollywood Agee did the scripts for *The African Queen* and *The Bride Comes to Yellow Sky*. But who remembers the author of even an unusual script? Still less fame was brought him by a script based on the life of Gauguin, "Noe Noe," since it has never been filmed. In 1951 Agee had his first coronary. From then until the year of his death he moved back and forth between California and New York. Television tempted him for a while; the script of the Ford Foundation "Omnibus" series on Abraham Lincoln was his.

But the medium was too young and restless to be able to use much of his meticulous kind of work. Contracts were there for him, but they always stipulated that he should write what he regarded as tripe.

At the end of his life he had gone back to writing fiction.

The whole point of tracing out his career is that at the end of it Agee wrote a short novel, two short stories, and part of a longer novel, all of such quality as to bring home to the reader a realization of what this man could have left behind if his great gift had not been channeled off in other directions. If he had "kept his promise" by writing what was expected of him instead of what he most wanted to write, he would have had his paragraph in the histories of fiction. At Exeter and at Harvard he had started a novel and had turned out perhaps two dozen short stories, some of which make excellent reading even today. But so far as I know, he wrote little fiction after he left Harvard, and he returned to the form too late to leave a lasting public impression.

In 1951 Houghton Mifflin brought out *The Morning Watch*, a story too short to be properly called a novel. It traces the emotions of a preadolescent boy in an Episcopal school in Tennessee as he watches before the Sacrament on Good Friday morning. The bulk of it is an interior monologue, supported by a few necessary external descriptions. The material is all autobiography: the school is Saint Andrews, where Agee had spent several years; the names of the characters are hardly changed from those of certain of the people mentioned in the "Dedication" of *Permit Me Voyage*. Even the lad called "Hog Eye" Kelsey in the story is a youth who in real life at Saint Andrews was known as "Frog Eye." Agee was using fiction, quite clearly, to investigate his own past.

The story follows a boy's effort to attain the perfect contrition appropriate to the day. He kneels in the chapel, tortured by self-suspicion. How does he know whether what he feels is not merely what he knows he is supposed to feel? Is he really sorry for all his sins? Or is he faking something, playing a role for his own enjoyment? Wrack himself as he will he does not find an answer, and at the end of his time of watching he goes off swimming with two other boys, breaking the school's rule for the sake of companionship. It need not be added that the "central consciousness" of the story is Agee himself. This is another treatment of the theme of *Let Us Now Praise Famous Men:* how to act truly, how not to be phony, how to be honest. And as the new fiction in this sense continues the book on sharecropping, which in turn continues the "Dedication," it also leads into *A Death in the Family,* the long novel Agee was working on when he died.

A day or so before he died, Agee told a friend that he needed two months to finish *A Death in the Family.* From the text as edited by his widow and his publisher it is not clear whether he was planning to add to the present twenty chapters or meant rather to spend the time reworking what he had already written. But the book as we have it is a series of scenes which tell a complete story, whether or not it is exactly the story Agee set out to tell.

A man named Jay Follet returns from a movie where he has been watching William S. Hart and Charlie Chaplin with his five- or six-year-old son Rufus. During the night a telephone call summons him: his father has had a heart attack. He says goodbye to his wife and drives out from Knoxville to his parents' home in one of the hill towns. He finds out that his father is in less danger than he had been told, his drunken brother having misled him. Here the story switches back to Knoxville, where the boy Rufus is taken shopping by an aunt on the morning after the telephone call. At ten the next evening Mary Follet, Rufus' mother, gets another

call, telling her to send some man out to a place along the
road where Jay has been in an accident. Mary's family gather
about her and wait in rising anxiety until they are sure that
Jay's accident has been fatal—which they finally learn is the
case. The rest of the main story (there are two flashbacks
which are not directly a part of it) studies the effect of Jay's
death on Mary's family from the time the word comes to the
end of the funeral. The family includes Rufus and his sister
Catherine, Mary's brother Andrew, the grandparents Joel
and (again) Catherine, and a great-aunt.

This was Agee's family, with some of the names not even
changed. Rufus was Agee's own middle name. James Agee,
"my brave father" as he calls him in the "Dedication," died in
an accident in 1915. In revising, he might have changed the
names, but he could not have disguised the family relationships. In the course of his protracted self-investigation, this
family situation simply imposed itself on him as a subject.
He felt that some of the conflicts in his own makeup could
be traced back to the mixture of strains in his blood, the
strain from the hills and the strain from the city; other conflicts he associated with the tension in the Knoxville family
between the extremely religious women and the skeptical,
somewhat tortured men. The father's death was a crucial
point because it had turned him, Agee, over completely to
his mother's family. But, at the same time, as material for
fiction this situation had inherent difficulties.

Whereas *Let Us Now Praise Famous Men* could be direct,
introspective reporting, and. *The Morning Watch* could be
handled through the stream of consciousness of a hero old
enough to understand something of what was happening to
him, Rufus is too young to serve as a "point-of-view" character. Moreover, the nature of the story is such that no character in it could report all the scenes on his own authority.
And Agee himself, at the time of his father's death, can

hardly have grasped the meaning of what went on about him. *A Death in the Family* thus had to be a reconstruction, built by projecting back to 1915 the various personalities, relationships, frictions, and affections that he had been able to observe later in his life.

The two flashbacks (in one of them his father comes to comfort him on a night when he cannot sleep; in the other the father drives the car when Rufus is taken to visit a centenarian great-great-grandmother) are much closer to direct reminiscence and make the nature of the scenes which are *not* flashback quite evident. The flashbacks serve to establish the novelist's relation to his material—and it is quite possible that if he had lived to do it Agee would have added more of them, corresponding to his feelings toward characters who do not enter the flashbacks we actually have.

I do not want to believe that he would have spent the two months he said he needed in turning this story into one of those housebroken novels that sophomores learn to write these days in college English classes. This could have been done by using various retrospective dodges, and time-manipulations such as would let Rufus learn later what at the time he had not known or had only dimly understood. But part of his job, as he had set it up for himself, was to feel his way into character after character, some of whom were as far away from the center of the story as his father's brother Ralph—who appears in it, really, only to make a telephone call. A novel which permits such multiplicity of interest has to be unified by something other than an intricate narrative method designed to maintain, in spite of all obstacles, a "consistent point of view." And in fact Agee had found his own way of preserving unity.

He could be intricate when he wanted, as anyone who has followed his early writing and particularly his verse can testify. But in *A Death in the Family* the intricacy shows up not in the arrangement of perspective but in the handling of minute detail, usually visual.

The wagon grew larger and larger, and now the dark, deeply lined faces of the man and woman became distinct; the sad, deeply lined faces of the profound country which seemed ancient even in early maturity and which always gave Jay a sense of peace. The woman sat high above the mule; the flare of her deep bonnet had the shape of the flare of the wagon's canopy. The man stood beside the wagon, one clayed boot cocked on the clayed hub. They gazed gravely into the eyes of the men on the ferry, and neither of them moved, or made any sign of salutation, until the craft was made fast.

It seems almost superfluous to insist here that this handling of visual detail, which at first seems remarkably casual, is, on the contrary, very highly organized. The eye of the narration moves toward the wagon; gets near enough to pick up the faces; dwells on them a moment; flicks up to the woman; identifies the similarity of bonnet and wagon canopy; moves down and sideways to the man; registers, balancing symmetrically with the identification of woman and wagon, the clay on the man's boot repeated by the clay on the wheel's hub. One thinks immediately of the kind of selection of detail that characterizes Agee's movie scripts, the secret of which is an inordinate capacity for revealing significance in a gesture, an object, any unobtrusive thing which seems only to "happen" to catch the eye. And as one contemplates the effect of a passage like this one about the wagon, and how the effect is obtained, one gradually realizes that here is something very rare: *A Death in the Family* is the opposite of a novel written *for* Hollywood; it brings a technique of script-writing, perhaps the essential technique of script-writing, to the writing of a novel.

There is no way, of course, to illustrate the function of this kind of vision in the novel as a whole; quotation would show how it works, but not how steadily, and its steadiness is what makes it so valuable. But anyone who reads the book at all alertly will, I believe, recognize its peculiar quality. The selecting, narrating vision moves through scene after scene, like the lens of a camera directed by someone who knows what the directors of the old silent films had to know if they were to survive: how to narrate visually. The consistent vision creates a tone common to all the scenes, obviates most of the need for transitions between them, holds the novel together. If a novelist must have a method, then this way of seeing was what constituted Agee's.

It does not, as do many techniques merely borrowed from Hollywood—all of them forms of ellipsis—produce an accelerated "pace." Where the filmed story handles events, dialogue, commentary, and psychological obbligati simultaneously, the written text has to treat them as successive. This is why the script of a movie takes longer to read than the film itself does to see, and why Agee's prose seems so leisurely and his scenes so emotionally complete, so thoroughly worked out.

A novel which leans as heavily upon autobiography as this one does would not have been sufficient to establish Agee as a novelist of first rank, even though we remember how much the Sartoris family means to Faulkner, and how often members of the authors' clans turn up in the fictions of Hemingway and Wolfe. We do not know that if he had lived to finish this novel he would have attempted fiction again. What A Death in the Family does demonstrate, very thoroughly, is that Agee had the equipment of a very considerable novelist, and of a very original one from the angle of technique. The question is whether he would ever have made much further use of the equipment. Given the special motive which led to his writing what little fiction he did in his maturity, the answer might very well have been negative.

Whenever Agee had to state his occupation, he simply put down "writer"—not journalist or novelist or poet. He was fully aware of how many different kinds of writing could give him satisfaction, and of how little he wanted to give himself to one, excluding the others. If he had wanted to pour his prose—and his almost embarrassing, indiscreet honesty—into, first, a novel about Harvard, then a novel about working for the Luce magazines, perhaps after that a novel about sharecroppers, and finally a novel about his family, he might have died at forty-five a well-known man and a "loss to American letters." But the truth is that with all the different possibilities open, he did not want to choose one and put the rest aside. So long as America invites talents to disperse as his did, fewer and fewer writers will be likely to face up to such a choice.

In other words, the men who could be our major novelists may be going . . . elsewhere.

Index